My mother knows Noël Coward

NOEL COWARD
AND HIS FRIENDS

NOEL COWARD

AND HIS FRIENDS

Cole Lesley, Graham Payn & Sheridan Morley

Designed by Craig Dodd

William Morrow and Company, Inc., New York

ACKNOWLEDGEMENTS

Illustrations have been reproduced with the kind help of and by courtesy of the following people, to whom the authors are most grateful: Cecil Beaton; Lord Snowdon; Harvard Theatre Collection (photos Angus McBean); Maurice Beck & MacGregor; Horst Tappe; National Film Archive; Pic Photos; Robert Penn; the Daily Express; Friedman-Abeles; Hewison; Paul Wilson; Matthew's News and Photo Agency; National Portrait Gallery, London; John Jensen; Erling Mandelmann/Comet; David Sim; Associated Newspapers; William Claxton; Pictorial Press; Mander and Mitchenson Theatre Collection; Victoria & Albert Museum, Enthoven Collection (photos Angelo Hornak and P. J. Gates Ltd); the New Yorker; Irene Koppel; Bill Young; Chappell & Co. Ltd; Douglas Weaver; Sasha, London; Emelie Danielson; Camera Press; The Tatler (and Bystander); Underwood & Underwood; Robert Davol; Vicky; Emmwood; Punch; Garrick Club, London; Derek Hill; Clemence Dane; Dasto; Honeyman; and Mrs Joan Hirst. Whilst the authors and publisher have made every effort to ensure that due acknowledgement has been made, it has not always been possible to trace the source of material from Noël Coward's albums and any error or omission will gladly be rectified in future editions.

First published in Great Britain by
Weidenfeld & Nicolson Ltd
91 Clapham High Street
London SW4 7TF
1979

Picture editor and designer Craig Dodd

Library of Congress Catalog Card Number 79-88008

ISBN 0-688-03510-8

Filmset and printed in Great Britain by
BAS Printers Limited, Over Wallop, Hampshire

CONTENTS

Lillian Gish wrote: 'I have lived long enough now to know
that the whole truth is never told in history texts.
Only the people who lived through an era,
who are the real participants in the drama as it occurs, know the
truth.'

With the help of his mother's reminiscences and his own journals,
all of which are as yet unpublished,
this is what the three of us, who between us knew Noël
so well for so long, have set out to do:
to tell the truth as we know it.

Cole Lesley
Graham Payn
Sheridan Morley

PREFACE

I
THE
BOY ACTOR

I cannot remember
I cannot remember
The house where I was born
But I know it was in Waldegrave Road
Teddington, Middlesex
Not far from the border of Surrey
An unpretentious abode
Which, I believe,
Economy forced us to leave
In rather a hurry.
But I *can* remember my grandmother's Indian shawl
Which, although exotic to behold,
Felt cold.
Then there was a framed photograph in the hall
Of my father wearing a Norfolk jacket,
Holding a bicycle and a tennis racquet
And leaning against a wall
Looking tenacious and distinctly grim
As though he feared they'd be whisked away from him.
I can also remember with repulsive clarity
Appearing at a concert in aid of charity
At which I sang, not the 'Green Hill Far Away' that you know
But the one by Gounod.
I remember a paper-weight made of quartz
And a sombre Gustave Doré engraving
Illustrating The Book of Revelations
Which, I am told, upset my vibrations.
I remember too a most peculiar craving
For liquorice all-sorts.
Then there was a song 'Oh That We Two Were Maying'
And my uncle, who later took to the bottle, playing
And playing very well
An organ called 'The Mustel'.
I remember the smell of rotting leaves
In the autumn quietness of suburban roads
And seeing the winter river flooding
And swirling over the tow-path by the lock.
I remember my cousin Doris in a party frock
With broderie anglaise at the neck and sleeves
And being allowed to stir the Christmas pudding
On long ago, enchanted Christmas Eves.
All this took place in Teddington, Middlesex
Not far from the Surrey border
But none of these little episodes
None of the things I call to mind
None of the memories I find
Are in chronological order
Is in chronological order.

Noël Coward

BUT NOËL'S MOTHER, MRS VIOLET COWARD, REMEMBERED THE house very well. It was a cosy little house called Helmsdale, she tells us, where she and her husband Arthur had lived since their marriage in 1891.

Mrs Coward must have been inspired to write her thirty-five foolscap pages of reminiscences of Noël's childhood and youth by the Treasure of Famous Children Exhibition in 1931, for she left in her trunk a large manila envelope addressed to The Organizing Secretary, St Stephen's House, Westminster, containing every single souvenir she had treasured of her own Famous Child since his birth. The more important of these treasures are reproduced in these pages; among them was a little blue book with *Baby's Record* in gold letters on the cover. From this we learn that Noël Peirce Coward was born at 2.30 a.m. on 16 December 1899, that his eyes were blue, his hair golden brown, and he weighed seven and a half pounds. 'I was looking forward with joy and longing to my little newcomer, little knowing the great happiness and pride I was to have in him, and how he was to alter all our lives. It seems almost incredible to think that I should have been destined to be the mother of a genius, but as it happens, I *am*!' Mrs Coward had amused herself for some time before by preparing Noël's nursery. 'I decorated a large white toy-cupboard in the style much favoured in those days. I painted a scene with mountains and sea in oils, and stuck on a large cut-out branch of apple blossom with some little boys in blue smocks fishing in a pond and a lot of little ducks swimming about – so pretty and gay for him to look at. . . .'

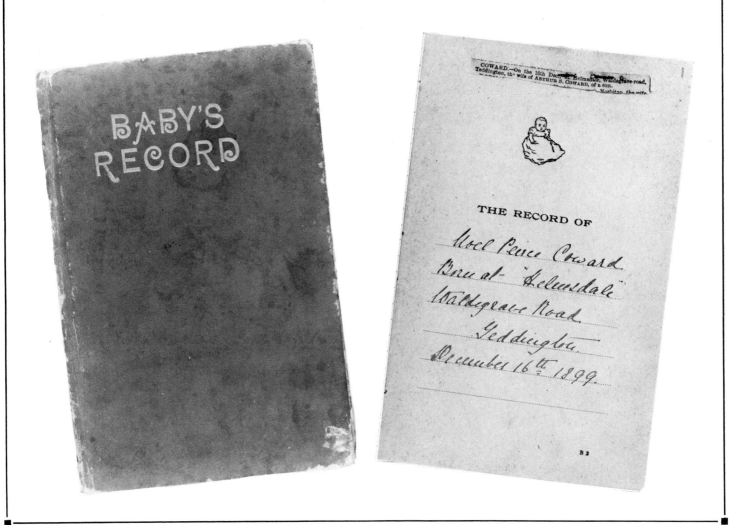

Noël's earliest achievements as faithfully recorded by his mother in 1900–1902; 'He was big for his age always', she wrote later, 'and very forward and amusing.'

Mrs Coward was evidently a fervent theatre-goer from her youth, for she saved all the programmes of the plays she saw, notably many starring Henry Irving and Ellen Terry at the Lyceum. And like her husband Arthur, she was very musical indeed: they had met and become engaged during the choir practices at the church of St Alban's, Teddington, where they were married and Noël was baptised. Arthur possessed 'a light tenor voice of great sweetness', Violet played the piano, and no less than fourteen members of the Coward family sang in the choir, as well as taking the leading parts in more secular productions at the Town Hall such as *The Gondoliers,* in which Violet 'tra-la-la'd demurely in the chorus'. This intensely musical atmosphere in which Noël spent all his childhood must surely have greatly influenced his musical development. His father, who at this time worked for Metzler's, the music publishers, loved to improvise at the piano. Noël, therefore, slipped easily into this pleasant and for him exciting way of passing the time, and in consequence had no formidable barrier to overcome when he started to compose his own songs and operettes.

The little family was happy, and sufficiently well-off to afford a maid-of-all-work named Emma, whose duties included helping with Noël, taking him for outings in his pram and warmly influencing his upbringing in those first formative years. 'My beloved old nurse Emma', it was, who said, 'You're too sharp by half: you'll cut yourself one of these days' – a warning Noël never forgot, though he did not always heed it.

This cheerful state of affairs lasted five years, after which the family

Arthur Sabin Coward, Noël's father; described as a 'clerk' on his marriage certificate, he later became a piano salesman for Metzler's. Violet Agnes (Veitch) Coward, Noël's mother; though not the traditional 'showbiz mum', her attitude to Noël was nonetheless both deeply loving and ambitious. In him, at a very early age, she recognized the successful one of the family.

fortunes declined. They moved first to a smaller house in Sutton, Surrey, where Noël's brother Eric was born; Mr Coward left Metzler's and 'travelled' for Payne's pianos, presumably selling them on commission, so that his income became precariously uncertain. Mrs Coward – always a realist – decided after three years that something must be done to help to clothe and feed the children, and so they moved again, this time to a top-floor flat overlooking Battersea Park, where she took in two young gentlemen as lodgers.

From the age of four onwards Noël had been in constant demand to sing and dance, at first in private, then in school and church concerts, or at church fêtes. Even when on holiday at the seaside he would enter the Kiddies' Competitions with the Concert Party on the sands and win them. He sang beautifully and danced violently, he says, 'with an assurance nothing short of petrifying'. The applause was deafening at his first public concert at the age of seven, his mother writes, 'and when there were cries of "Encore!" he leaned over to me in the front row and said delightedly "That means I've got to sing again!" and to everyone's astonishment climbed on to the piano stool and accompanied himself singing a sweet little Australian song *Time To Rise*. He was quite the success of the evening.'

He had, therefore, more than enough poise and experience to face an

The young Master, alone and with his only brother Eric (an elder brother had died before Noël's birth). 'Destiny's Tot', as Woollcott later called Noël, grew up in a succession of suburban south London homes and showed an early determination to join the more theatrically-inclined members of his family, many of whom were in church choirs and one of whom was known as 'the Twickenham Nightingale'.

THE LITTLE THEATRE

JOHN STREET, ADELPHI, STRAND.

Manageress ... ... GERTRUDE KINGSTON

FRIDAY, JANUARY 27th at 2.30

AND EVERY TUESDAY & FRIDAY AFTERNOON

LILA FIELD'S

CHILDREN'S THEATRE MATINEES

— THE —

GOLDFISH

A FAIRY PLAY, IN THREE ACTS,

BY LILA FIELD

... WITH A ...

STAR CAST OF WONDER CHILDREN

PRICES OF ADMISSION:—

Private Boxes, £2 2s. and £1 1s. Orchestra Stalls, 10s. 6d. and 7s. 6d. Stalls, 5s. and 2s. 6d.
(For these Performances only).

ALL SEATS ARE RESERVED, AND CAN BE BOOKED IN ADVANCE AT BOX OFFICE

W. T. Haycock & Co. (1909), Ltd., Printers, Dean Street, Soho.

14

September 7, 1910

LONDON THEATRE FOR CHILDREN.

Juvenile Actors and Actresses in Adventure Plays.

MISS LILA FIELD'S PLAN.

London is shortly to possess a "Children's Theatre," where none of the actors or actresses will be more than fourteen years old.

Miss Lila Field, who last winter most successfully presented at the Playhouse "The Goldfish," a play acted entirely by children, is the moving spirit in this enterprise. Miss Field gave *The Daily Mirror* an interesting outline of her scheme yesterday.

"My plays will begin in the middle of October," she said, "at one of the large West End theatres.

"It is more than probable that a piece will be running at the theatre in the usual way. But on five afternoons in every week the house will become the 'Children's Theatre,' and these plays acted by children will be presented there.

SEARCH FOR CHILD ACTORS.

"For many months past now I have been busy collecting my cast; as I want thirty or so bright children between the ages of ten and fourteen this has been far from an easy task.

"To get suitable boys has been especially difficult. I have got sufficient girls at last, but am still badly in need of five or six boys."

ROYAL COURT THEATRE
SLOANE SQUARE.

Monday, April 17th, 1911, for Six Nights

Miss LILA FIELD'S Company "The Goldfish"

SPECIAL MATINEES

Wednesday, Thursday and Saturday, April 19th, 20th and 22nd

Sept: 11th ....

Many thanks for your letter, I shall be pleased to see your little son, on Tuesday next at *10.45* at my studio –
24. King Street.
Baker Street. W

Y^{rs} v. truly
Lila Field:

The Boy Actor: the Daily Mirror's *account in July 1910 of Lila Field's search for children that could act was spotted by Mrs Coward, who took Noël along to an audition. What the programme described as a 'Star Cast of Wonder Children' also included Ninette de Valois, June and a Master Alfred Willmore, later better known as Micheál MacLiammóir.*

Daily Mirror

January 28, 1911

CAST OF CHILDREN.

Young Actors in Charming Play Chosen from Applicants to "Daily Mirror."

Before a delighted audience at the Little Theatre yesterday afternoon Miss Lila Field's company of child actors and actresses made their first bow to the public in "The Goldfish."

This was the first performance of what Miss Lila Field hopes to be permanent children's theatre matinées. In time it is hoped that a school for boy and girl actors will be opened in connection with these performances.

All the boys and several of the girls who played in "The Goldfish" yesterday were obtained through the agency of *The Daily Mirror*. Last September Miss Field, in an interview with *The Daily Mirror*, stated that she wanted a few boy and girl actors.

On the day following the publication of the interview over 200 applications from would-be boy and girl actors were received at *The Daily Mirror* Office, and from these a selection was made.

The story of "The Goldfish" is extremely simple. A party of children playing on the sea shore visit a cave, where they become transformed to starfishes, anemones, mussels, soles and other fishes.

Great success was scored by Master Noel Coward as Prince Mussel, while Master Burford Hampden, as King Starfish, created great amusement.

Other little actors and actresses who distinguished themselves were Kathleen Ross-Lyell, Beatrice Beauchamp (a delightful dancer) and Nellie Terriss.

Youngest of the actors who played in "The Goldfish" was Master Eric Lascelles, aged ten, who acted with great confidence and spirit.

Vida Veitch, Noël's mother's sister, with whom the Coward family went to stay one pre-war summer at Lee-on-Solent, a visit Auntie Vida repaid almost ever afterwards.

audition for his first professional appearance with self-assurance at the age of ten. On 7 September 1910, 'when we were at breakfast, Noël found an advertisement in the *Daily Mirror* asking for a bright boy to take a principal part in a children's play, and worried me to answer it'. (By the time Noël and his mother wrote their separate recollections of this momentous morning, more than twenty years later, they had both come firmly to believe what they wrote; Noël repeated the story in innumerable interviews over many years until the 'advertisement' became world-famous. However, the most careful searching of the *Daily Mirror* files revealed no such advertisement. The accurate evidence had been lying, forgotten for more than sixty years, at the bottom of what Noël came to call 'Mum's suitcase' of souvenirs.) What Noël read aloud that morning was, in fact, an interview with a Miss Lila Field, who had written, and had already produced a year earlier at the Playhouse, a musical play for children called *The Goldfish*. She planned to produce it again that autumn, and hoped to found a permanent London Theatre for Children: 'To get suitable boys has been especially difficult. I have got sufficient girls at last, but am still badly in need of five or six boys.' This was, of course, more than enough for Noël to urge his mother to write to Miss Field care of the *Daily Mirror,* though she says she expected nothing to come of it. The *Mirror* received more than two hundred letters the next morning from similarly eager mothers, and by happy chance or exceptional acumen Mrs Coward's was among the comparative few they selected to forward to Miss Field. Four mornings later a postcard arrived; 'Many thanks for your letter. I shall be pleased to see your little son on Tuesday next at 10.45 at my studio, 24 King Street, Baker Street, W.I. Yrs v. truly, Lila Field'.

I can't tell you the excitement Noël was in, and indeed I was too. Off we went on the top of a bus and presently found ourselves in a large room with a grand piano, then Miss Field came in – I liked her, she was refined and looked clever. She asked Noël to recite, which he did, and tears came into her eyes she was so excited about him. Her sister arrived and Noël sang *There Is A Green Hill Far Away* and they both passed out. When Miss Field came to terms, she said, "It will be a guinea and a half a week", and I immediately thought she wanted me to pay that, but she said, "He will *receive* that", and we thought his fortune was made!'

Mrs Coward, splendid in grey satin and a feather boa, and Noël, exhilarated in his new Norfolk suit with an Eton collar, buoyantly descended the stairs into the street and thence to Selfridge's, where, over gala ice-cream sodas, they tried to calculate the astronomical amount of money he would earn in a year. They were overcome with joy and astonishment when they opened the *Mirror* the morning after the first performance to find no fewer than four photographs of the 'Star Cast of Wonder Children', and the magical wording of Noël's first professional press notice – 'Great success is scored by Master Noël Coward'.

Four of the Wonder Children were destined for fame: Noël, Ninette de Valois, Micheál MacLiammóir, and 'Little June' Tripp, a radiantly fair and pretty girl, later to become famous as 'June', star of many 1920s musical comedies. June has described Noël at this point as a boy with elfin ears and a foul temper. 'My aversion to Noël, with his black suits [at rehearsals], horse-laughter and fiendish grimaces was expressed in haughty head-tossings. Many years later Noël explained our juvenile antipathy with Cowardian conciseness and clipped diction: "Brrattish rreaction to each other's brrilliance, darling!"'

Micheál MacLiammóir, too, has left his impression of Noël at *The Goldfish* rehearsals, here abridged:

He was ten years old and already in manner and bearing a young man. The face, of course, was that of a child but the eyes were already amused and slightly incredulous, the voice was as crisply *rubato* then as it is today, and when he spoke after a few preliminary boyish grins it was to ask me how much work I had done.

'Work?' I said aghast. 'Do you mean acting?'

'But you've had your audition, haven't you?'

'Oh yes, I'm engaged,' and then ... 'What are you going to be when you grow up?'

'An actor of course. Why, what do you want to be?'

Micky was not at all sure.

'You'd better make up your mind, you know. People should always be quite clear about what they want to be.'

Remembering Mrs Coward's love of going to the theatre before her marriage, it should be stressed that she went as often as she possibly could all through Noël's boyhood, taking him with her as an ideal companion. 'He went to his first theatre, a pantomime at Kingston, when he was just four years old. ... He and I used to go to matinées whenever there was anything suitable on, like a revue or musical comedy, and he did so love it. I never thought it over-excited him; he sat quite quietly all the time, watching.' At the age of seven these outings became even more thrilling for Noël, for from then onwards they were always to much more glamorous theatres in the West End. The pit was the most they could afford, and to attain the front row by dint of queueing early was perfect bliss. Those were the days of great stars in hugely successful musicals, and Noël idolized Lily Elsie in *The Merry Widow* and Gertie Millar in *The Quaker Girl* – or anything else either of them ever did, in fact. 'I was taken to *The King*

Right: St Alban's in Teddington, the church of Noël's christening, was also the scene of some of his earliest appearances.

An Autumn Idyll ('to music', said the programme, 'by F. Chopin') was a Ruby Ginner ballet in which Miss Ginner herself appeared as an Autumn Leaf ('rather too large to be blown about by the wind', wrote Noël) and Master Coward himself was billed as a Mushroom.

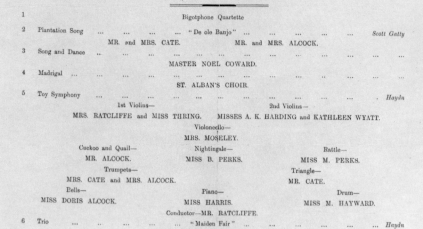

The Times of 26 June 1912: 'Master Coward headed delightfully a little troupe of small but engaging fungi'. It failed to note, however, that Master Eric Coward's name was also to be found in the programme, though in rather smaller lettering, as one of the other toadstools.

SAVOY THEATRE.
Licensed by the Lord Chamberlain to
Mr. G. A. Richardson (Secretary Savoy Theatre and Opera, Ltd.), Savoy Hotel, W.C.

Every Evening at 8.15. Matinees Wednesday & Saturday 2.15.
LAST WEEK FOR THIS SEASON.
Mr. CHARLES HAWTREY'S PRODUCTION.

WHERE THE RAINBOW ENDS

By CLIFFORD MILLS and JOHN RAMSEY
Music specially composed by Mr. ROGER QUILTER.

Characters
(in the order of their appearance)

Rosamund Carey	...	Miss ESME WYNNE
Crispian Carey	...	Master PHILIP TONGE
William	...	Master NOEL COWARD
Cubs	...	Master GUIDO CHIARLETTI
Matilda Flint	...	Miss JEANNIE THOMAS
Joseph Flint	...	Mr. C. W. SOMERSET
Schlapps	...	Mr. HENRY MORRELL
The Genie of the Carpet	...	Master SIDNEY SHERWOOD
Jim Blunders	...	Miss DOT TEMPLE
Betty Blunders	...	Mr. REGINALD OWEN
	...	Mr. CLIFTON ALDERSON
	...	Miss MAVIS YORKE
	...	Mr. REGINALD P. LAMB
	...	Miss MAXINE HINTON
	...	Mr NORMAN MACOWAN
	...	Miss LYDIA BILBROOKE
	...	Master HARRY DUFF
	...	Mr. MAURICE TOSH
	...	Miss GRACE SEPPINGS
	...	Mr. J. K. EDRO
	...	Miss ZOE GORDON

Flower Fairies, Dragon Flies, Rainbow Children,
Caterpillars, Toads, a Leopard, etc.

... Sepping, Isla Raine, Rosie Block, Ruth Block.
... and Rainbow Children—Ivy Bell, Edna
Jones, Eileen Grist, Rita Vivian, Irene Birch,
a Warneford, Margaret Stuart, Dorothy Moody,
ithey, Joyce Robey, etc.

etc.—Leslie Ryecroft, Reginald Grawdorf, Philip
Norman Haddock, Jack Rea, John Renshaw,
unsard, Frank Bates, Jim Taylor, Sidney Spiro,
ht, William Wodehouse, John Dixon, Arthur

ghton, Arthur Grayson, Charles Gordon,
Stanley Ramsden, etc.

Children trained by Miss ITALIA CONTI.

Synopsis of Scenery.

ACT I.	Scene 1.	Library at Riversdale, Maidenhead (*Evening*)
	Scene 2.	The Flight of the Carpet
ACT II.	Scene 1.	The Outskirts of the Dragon's Wood
ACT III.	Scene 1.	The Witch's Cove
	Scene 2.	The Dragon Wood (*Evening*)
	Scene 3.	The Lake at the end of the Wood (*Night*)
ACT IV.	Scene 1.	Ramparts of Dragon's Castle on topmost crag of Thundercloud Mountains
	Scene 2.	"Where the Rainbow Ends" (Where All Lost Loved Ones are Found)

Scenery designed by Mr. TOM HESLEWOOD and Painted by ALFRED E. CRAVEN.

Dresses designed by Mr. TOM HESLEWOOD and Executed by
L. & H. NATHAN and Miss VIOLET MURRAY.
Animal Costumes by Messrs. ELKAN BROS. and FRED C. LABHART.
Furniture by J. S. LYON.   Wigs by CLARKSON.
Flying Effects by HAROLD ROSS.   Electrical Effects by T. J. DIGBY.
Theatre Decorations by A. and L. UHLMANN.

Music published by ELKIN & Co., of 8 and 10 Beak Street, W.

The Play Produced by Mr. CHARLES HAWTREY.

Musical Director	(For Mr. Hawtrey)	Mr. W. JACKSON BYLES
Stage Director	"	Mr. B. CAMLIN SMITH
Stage Manager	"	Mr. OSWALD STRONG
Assistant Stage Manager	"	Mr. LESLIE RYECROFT
Business Manager	(For Savoy Theatre)	Mr. HARRY P. TOWERS

Private Boxes, £5 5s.; £3 3s. & £2 2s.   Stalls, 10s. 6d.   Balcony Stalls, 7s. 6d.
First Circle (Reserved), Front Row, 5s.; other Rows, 4s.   Pit, 2s. 6d. Gallery, 1s.
Box Office (Mr. RICHARD WEAVER) open from 10 a.m. till 10 p.m.
Telephone: 2602 GERRARD.   Telegrams: "Newsavo, London."

General Manager ... (For Mr. Hawtrey) ... Mr. EDWARD FITZGERALD

THE SAVOY RESTAURANT.

The THEATRE and RESTAURANT are in direct communication with
each other UNDER COVER.
Take the Pass Staircase leading from the Theatre Vestibule at the
Embankment level to the new Theatre Entrance at the Strand level.

DINNERS à la carte. | SUPPERS after the Theatre,
(Menus from 12.6 per person and upwards.) | à prix fixe, 5/6
The beautiful NEW ANNEXE to the Foyer and Restaurant is NOW OPEN.

Where The Rainbow Ends, *that annual entry in every child actor's diary of the period: Noël played William in 1911 and 1912, before graduating to* Peter Pan, *and the* Birmingham Post *considered that he 'played a thankless part with much skill and effect'. Philip Tonge – also in that 1911 cast – was to turn up in American telecasts of Coward plays as late as the mid-1950s.*

N.B.—This Form must accompany any inquiry respecting this Telegram.

POST OFFICE TELEGRAPHS.

...ver of an Inland Telegram doubts its accuracy, he may have it ...peated on payment of half the
...ion, any fraction of 1d. less than ½d. being reckoned as ½d.; and if it be found that there was any
...will be refunded. Special conditions are applicable to the repetition of Foreign Telegrams.

TO Noel Coward Savoy Theatre
Best of good luck and I hope a good hard
smack
Charles Hawtrey

Letters home: by now the family were living at Sutton in Surrey, but Noël would go for summer holidays to stay with his Aunt Laura near St Austell in Cornwall.

of Cadonia on my ninth birthday and fell in love with Gracie Leigh.' He developed at this time the remarkable gift of going straight to the piano when they got home and playing the greater part of the score from memory, with the correct harmonies. Small wonder that Noël's intensely musical family background, combined with his longing to act, sing or dance for any willing audience, and his careful 'watching' and absorbing all he saw when at the theatre, led to his having become a professional actor by the age of ten. It was inevitable.

'Miss Field's children had made a name for themselves, they were considered clever', and Mrs Coward, though delighted, seems not to have been unduly surprised that the great Charles Hawtrey should send for Noël to appear with him in his autumn production, *The Great Name,* in which Noël played a page-boy. Charles Hawtrey was the most brilliant light comedian of his time, capable too of playing with moving tenderness when called upon. Noël hero-worshipped him, and off and on served a seven year 'apprenticeship' with him, during which he learnt most of what there was to know about acting, and a great deal about the craft of playwriting. Noël took great pride in the good fortune he'd had of acting with Hawtrey and never forgot how much he owed him.

At the end of this same year, 1911, Hawtrey again asked Noël to play in the very first production of *Where The Rainbow Ends,* a charming fairy-tale with music, which came to be so much loved by the public that it was revived at almost every Christmas-time for the next forty years or so. Noël appeared three times in it, and twice in that other perennial and much-loved favourite *Peter Pan.* He adored both plays and playing in them, and he looked back on these years with happy nostalgia.

I can remember, I can remember,
The months of November and December
   Were filled for me with peculiar joys
So different from those of other boys.
   For other boys would be counting the days
Until end of term and holiday times,
   But I was acting in Christmas plays
While they were taken to pantomimes.
   I didn't envy their Eton suits,
Their children's dances and Christmas trees.
   My life had wonderful substitutes
For such conventional treats as these.
   I didn't envy their country larks,
Their organised games in panelled halls:
   While they made snow men in stately parks
I was counting the curtain calls.

I can remember. I can remember.
The months of November and December,
   Although climatically cold and damp,
Meant more to me than Aladdin's lamp.
   I see myself, having got a job,
Walking on wings along the Strand,
   Uncertain whether to laugh or sob
And tightly clutching my mother's hand.
   I never cared who scored the goal
Or which side won the silver cup,
   I never learned to bat or bowl
But I heard the curtain going up.

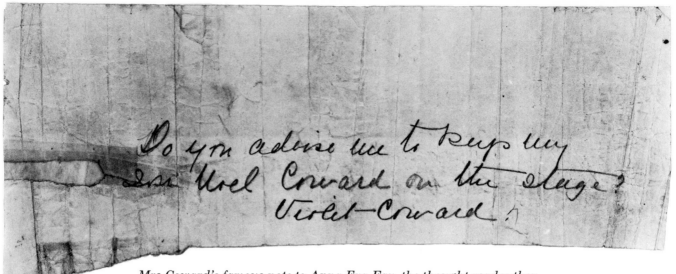

Mrs Coward's famous note to Anna Eva Fay, the thought-reader then topping the bill at the Coliseum, enquiring about her son's future. 'Keep him where he is!' came the reply; 'He will have a wonderful career!'

Noël's childhood had on the whole been a most happy one: his only unhappinesses seem to have been caused by separations from his mother, as for instance when she decided to let the flat in Battersea and that the family should stay with his Grannie and two of his numerous aunts at Southsea. His education had been sporadic to say the least, which from time to time caused Mrs Coward pangs of conscience, and from Southsea she suddenly packed Noël off alone to London to stay with yet another aunt and continue his schooling.

'Dear darling old Mother, I am still very unhappy and I shan't get over it till I see you again . . . oh Mother do send me some money to come down to you please do I am not very happy here without you . . . good bye now darling old mother from your loveing son Noël, please do do do do send back for me.' This was written at the age of ten. Two years later, while Noël was appearing for the second time in *Where The Rainbow Ends,* she not only suffered further pangs of guilt but writes that she was 'a good deal pestered by relations and friends about letting Noël be on the stage instead of at school, and had doubts in my mind as to what was the wisest thing to do'.

An end was put to her indecision once and for all in a startling manner: a friend asked Mrs Coward to accompany her to a variety performance at the Coliseum, where a thought-reader, Anna Eva Fay, was topping the bill.

She had created a tremendous sensation in America and the Coliseum was packed. A man came round with slips of paper for you to write your question on. I was not going to ask anything but my friend persuaded me to. [The slip was later given back and can be seen in these pages – her question pencilled on very thin white paper, much folded and twisted in Mrs Coward's agitation] 'Do you advise me to keep my son Noël Coward on the stage? Violet Coward.' Then there was a hush and Miss Fay came on to the stage, with her male assistant. She spoke a few words, then sat on a chair and the man put a sheet over her. She held out her arms like a ghost, answered one or two questions and then called out 'Mrs Coward, Mrs Coward' – my friend prodded me in the side and I had to stand up and she shouted, 'You ask me about your son. Keep him where he is, keep him where he is, he has great talent and will have a wonderful career!' I was entirely flabbergasted . . . my feelings were beyond words, how could she know and *why* should she have answered me amongst so many people! When I mentioned my experience [to the relations] I was met with pitying smiles! So I did not say any more about it but I knew perfectly well that Anna Eva Fay was right.

And then she adds with an understandable little note of self-justification that Noël *did* get in some schooling during the year 1912. But not a lot.

In March 1913 Noël was asked by Italia Conti to appear in Liverpool and Manchester in Hauptmann's *Hannele*. His mother let him go unwillingly without her, but he was so thrilled and excited by the opportunity to play both a schoolboy and an angel that she allowed it. She saw him off at Euston on what was later to prove for him and for many thousands of people a momentous journey, for during it Noël Coward met Gertrude Lawrence for the first time. Gertie was fourteen to Noël's twelve and therefore infinitely more sophisticated and worldly, clad in a black satin coat and a hat with a peak, with a fund of naughty stories to tell, and blatantly powdering her nose in public when she wanted to, which was often. She gave Noël an orange, and from then on he felt he had become part of what he afterwards used to love to describe as 'the mad, mad world of powder and paint'.

The other ten or so young members of the cast included Harold French and a 'perky boy in a yachting cap' called Roy Royston. They had a jolly journey, eating sandwiches and chocolate, and playing card games. The action of *Hannele* takes place in a mountain village in Germany; Noël,

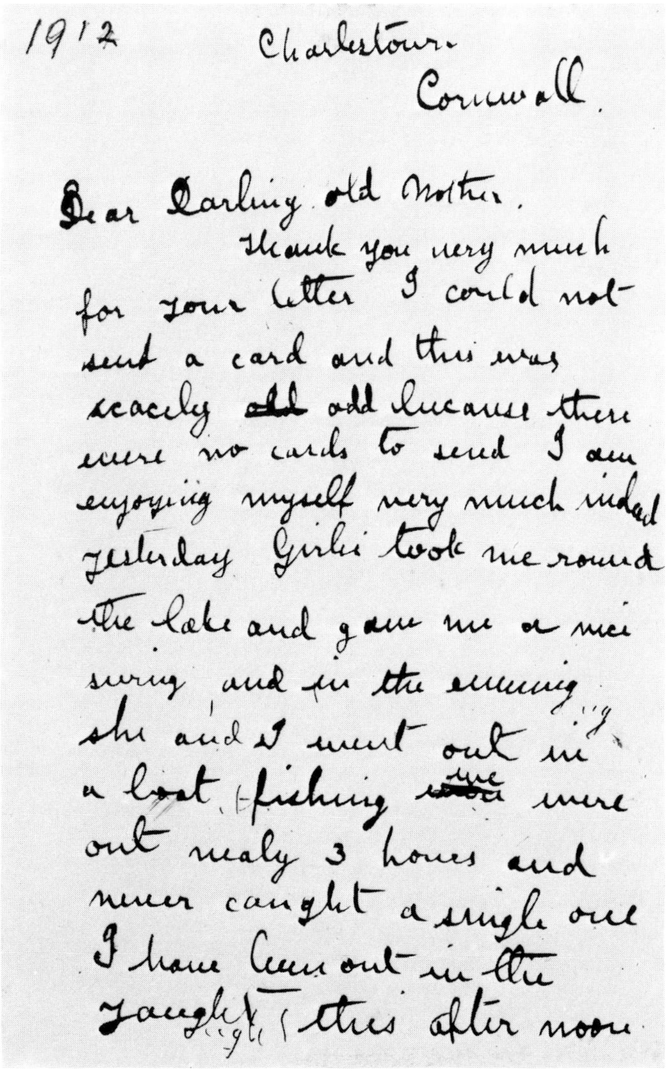

1912

Charlestown
Cornwall.

Dear Darling old Mother.
    thank you very much for your letter I could not send a card and this was scacely old odd because there were no cards to send I am enjoying myself very much indeed yesterday Girlie took me round the lake and gave me a nice swing and in the evening she and I went out in a boat fishing we were out nealy 3 hours and never caught a single one I have been out in the yaught this after noon

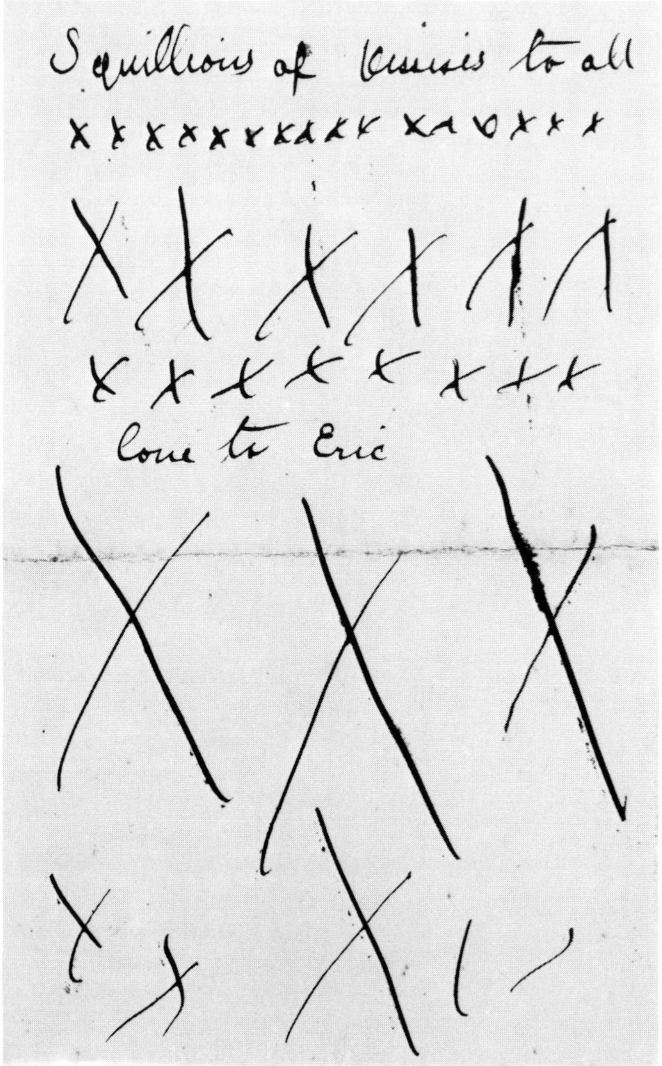

Squillions of kisses to all
X X X X X X K X X X X X X X X X

X X X X X
X X X X X X X X
love to Eric

Dear and most august
parent,

This is a letter although
you may not think
so
————————

these lines are to show how much
I adore you

I am still as beautiful
as rotten mangold-Wurzel.
I met the Douglas
woman to-day and told
her what fun I had
when I was at my
Zenith! (I hope that isent
a rude word !!!)

Farewell Beloved

Your

Sweet . .

Son

NOEL

Harold and Roy were schoolboys, then transformed into Angels of Light at the end of the first part and whisked off to a sort of dream heaven in the second, where Baliol Holloway, their schoolmaster, had also been transfigured into 'the Stranger', who bore a remarkable resemblance to Jesus. Once the three angels got to heaven they came across Gertie, as a member of the Angelic Chorus. She and Noël behaved very badly, gravitating towards one another in the crowd so as not to miss one moment of the fun. They hugely enjoyed the matinée when Phyllis Williams came down the centre aisle of the theatre swinging her censer so wildly that it became unscrewed and a matronly lady stood up screaming and shaking hot ashes from her lap. Another time, while Mr Holloway was making his quick change back to being a schoolmaster, they heard a great deal of scuffling, effing and blinding coming from behind a ground row of box trees and Gertie whispered, 'Sounds to me as if Christ has lost his trousers.' Noël had found a new friend after his own heart, a friend for life.

While in Manchester, those children who were under fourteen and therefore had to have a licence to act were made to go to a police court, where a bad-tempered magistrate ordered them to attend school every day. This infuriated Noël, who announced to the teacher that he had no intention of answering any questions he might be asked and that, if he were caned or in any way punished, he would go straight home to London. From that morning on he sat at the back of the classroom quietly and happily reading a book of his own choice. And that is the last mention made of Noël's education.

By the time he was fifteen, he had grown too big to play the Pageboy in his last year of *Where The Rainbow Ends*; he was cast as the Slacker, a much more bravura part, half-man, half-dragon, which he played full out in blue and yellow make-up, his eyelids besequinned. As before, the leading rôle was played by Esmé Wynne, but it was not until this third production that their friendship became important to Noël, and even more important when they both obtained leading parts in the tour of *Charley's Aunt* during the spring and summer of 1915. Until he got to know her well, he had thought Esmé rather stodgy and she agreed with him that he looked rather podgy, and so the nicknames Stodge and Podge were evidently used by mutual consent. (It was not until later, when they were passing through their romantic *Cherry Pan* phase, that the more whimsical spellings Stoj and Poj were adopted.)

Esmé's consuming ambition was to become a writer and in this she succeeded, publishing some very well-reviewed novels. She seems to have been a natural writer in the sense that nothing could stop her writing, her pen racing over the pages. This impressed Noël enormously and it is impossible to exaggerate the influence she exerted over him at this time and in the ensuing years. His competitive spirit contributed; not to be outdone, he too started to write and from then on, like Esmé, never stopped writing until he died.

All through the tour of *Charley's Aunt* Stodge and Podge spent every waking moment together if they could, always trying to get into the same theatrical digs if possible, so that they could continue their non-stop arguments about life, sex, religion, Oscar Wilde and Bernard Shaw. The philosophy of *The Rubaiyat of Omar Khayyam* was much to their liking; the fact that it was (then) considered daring and, better still, pagan, made it all the more alluring and they longed to drink from the cup of life. But in this, more often than not, they were thwarted by the Company Manager Cecil Barth with his 'unbridled passion for respectability': he considered their close relationship improper. They thought nothing of taking their baths together; it would have been too silly to take them separately and waste minutes of their precious time, but Mr Barth feared they would give the company a bad name and saw to it that they at least did not sleep in the same lodgings.

To my friend Noel from P.S.S. 1914.

Summer holidays were still being spent either with Auntie Vida or else in Cornwall, where his artist friend Philip Streatfield had taken a house. They were together at Polperro when, on 4 August 1914, war was declared.

DUKE OF YORK'S THEATRE
ST. MARTIN'S LANE. :: W.C.

TUESDAY, DECEMBER 23rd, 1913, at 2 o'clock.

Proprietors ... ... Mr. & Mrs. Frank Wyatt
Sole Lessee and Manager ... CHARLES FROHMAN

CHARLES FROHMAN presents

PETER PAN
OR, THE BOY WHO WOULDN'T GROW UP

By J. M. BARRIE

The Music Composed and Arranged by JOHN CROOK

10TH YEAR

Peter Pan	...	PAULINE CHASE
Jas. Hook	...	GODFREY TEARLE
Mr. Darling	...	BASIL FOSTER
Mrs. Darling	...	NINA SEVENING
Wendy Moira Angela Darling	...	MARY GLYNNE
John Napoleon Darling	...	ALFRED WILLMORE
Michael Nicholas Darling	...	DONALD BUCKLEY
Nana	...	EDWARD SILLWARD
Tinker Bell	...	JANE WREN
Tootles		GERTRUDE LANG
Nibs		MARJORIE GRAHAM
Slightly	Members of Peter's Band	NOEL COWARD
Curly		PRUDENCE BOURCHIER
First Twin		DORIS McINTYRE
Second Twin		JOAN COULTHURST
Smee		GEORGE SHELTON
Gentleman Starkey		CHARLES TREVOR
Cookson		CHARLES MEDWIN
Mullins	Pirates	JAMES PRIOR
Cecco		WILLIAM LUFF
Jukes		JAMES ENGLISH
Noodler		JOHN KELT
		Messrs. A. STEVENSON, S. SPENCER and W. HARBERD
Great Big Little Panther	Redskins	HUMPHREY WARDEN
Tiger Lily		MARGARET FRASER

Braves, ANNA WALDEN, ALMA DUDLEY, MARGARET KING, GLADYS BRENDA, ETHEL WELLESLEY, TONIE EDGAR-BRUCE.

Mermaid	...	DORA SEVENING
Baby Mermaid	...	MOYA NUGENT
Liza	*(Author of the Play)*	MOYA NUGENT
Crocodile	...	D. BUCKLEY and F. W. CECIL
Ostrich	...	GORDON CARR

Pack of Wolves—E. GRATA, A. BROCKNOR, H. KENT, A. WILLMER, F. MILLER, GORDON CARR

CHARLES FROHMAN.
LONDON & NEW YORK.

DUKE OF YORK'S THEATRE,
Charles Frohman, Lessee & Manager.

Telegrams:- Ferry, London.
Telephone 1786 Gerrard.

ADDRESS ALL COMMUNICATIONS TO

GENERAL MANAGER,
W. LESTOCQ.

TRAFALGAR HOUSE,
WATERLOO PLACE,
S.W.

December 29th 1913

Master Noel Coward
50 South Side
CLAPHAM COMMON

Dear Master Coward,
On behalf of Mr Charles Frohman I engage you to play the part of "Slightly" in the revival of "Peter Pan" at the Duke of Yorks Theatre, on or about December 23rd, at a salary of £4 a week Kindly write and confirm this and oblige.

Yours truly,

Above: Peter Pan: *the engagement letter is evidently misdated (December for November) but the money is all too accurate.*

MONDAY, MARCH 31st, 1913, FOR SIX NIGHTS AT 7·30
MATINEE : SATURDAY AT 2
FIFTH VISIT OF THE LIVERPOOL REPERTORY COMPANY
Under the Direction of Mr. BASIL DEAN

SER TALDO'S BRIDE
A COMEDY BY BARRY JACKSON AND JOHN DRINKWATER
Produced by BASIL DEAN
Scene designed by GEORGE W. HARRIS
Petruccia's song specially composed for this production by ARNOLD CLIBBORN

(Characters in the order of their appearance)

Petruccia, a serving maid	...Miss ELLINOR ARUP
Father Galgano, the village priest	...Mr. J. H. ROBERTS
Ser Taldo, a professor	...Mr. WILFRID E. SHINE
Master Simone, a doctor of laws	...Mr. SHIEL BARRY
Madonna Fioretta	...Miss EILEEN THORNDIKE

SCENE—Outside a village inn in Italy
This play is founded upon an early Italian story

HANNELE
A DREAM-POEM BY GERHARDT HAUPTMANN
English Translation by WILLIAM ARCHER
Production by BASIL DEAN
Music specially composed for this production by ARNOLD CLIBBORN
The Dresses and Cottage Scene designed by GEORGE W. HARRIS
The Children trained by ITALIA CONTI, of London

(The characters in the order of their appearance)

Tulpe		Miss FANNY OLIVE	1st Mourner ...Miss NORA CHARRINGTON
Hedwig (known as Hete)	Inmates of a pauper refuge	Miss BEATRICE SMITH	2nd Mourner ...Miss KATHLEEN FITZSIMONS
Pleschke		Mr. WILFRID E. SHINE	3rd Mourner ...Miss MONA SMITH
Hanke		Mr. RICHARD EVANS	4th Mourner ...Miss DORIS LLOYD
Gottwald, a schoolmaster		Mr. BALIOL HOLLOWAY	5th Mourner ...Miss NINA HENDERSON
Seidel, a woodcutter		Mr. ALGERNON F. GREGG	Hanke ...Mr. RICHARD EVANS
Hannele, a poor waif		Miss GRACE SEPPINGS	Pleschke ...Mr. WILFRID E. SHINE
Schmidt, a police official		Mr. J. A. DODD	Seidel ...Mr. ALGERNON F. GREGG
Berger, an engineer		Mr. NORMAN McKEOWN	The Stranger ...Mr. BALIOL HOLLOWAY
Dr. Wachler		Mr. J. H. ROBERTS	1st Angel ...Miss EILEEN THORNDIKE
Sister Martha		Miss AIDA JENOURE	and Angel ...Miss ELLINOR ARUP
			Master ROY ROYSTON
(The figures in Hannele's dream-play in the order of their appearance)			Master NOEL COWARD
Mattern, a mason (reputed to be Hannele's father)		Mr. SHIEL BARRY	Miss EILEEN FRENCH
A female figure (Hannele's mother)		Miss MAIRE O'NEILL	Miss PHYLLIS WILLIAMS
		Master ROY ROYSTON	The Angelic Chorus Miss MARGERY WALKER
The Three Angels of Light		Master NOEL COWARD	Miss MARJORIE WITHEY
		Master HAROLD FRENCH	Miss DOROTHY MOODY
Two Censer Bearers		Miss MARGERY WALKER	Miss GERTRUDE LAWRENCE
		Miss PHYLLIS WILLIAMS	Miss MARGARET STEWART
The Angel of Death		Mr. NORMAN McKEOWN	Mr. JOHN COLLINS
A Sister of Mercy		Miss AIDA JENOURE	Four white-robed Youths Mr. HAROLD WALTON
The Village Tailor		Mr. SHIEL BARRY	Mr. ARTHUR CLEMENTS
Gottwald		Mr. BALIOL HOLLOWAY	Mr. ARTHUR C. ROSE
		Master ROY ROYSTON	
		Master NOEL COWARD	
Six School Children		Miss PHYLLIS WILLIAMS	
		Miss MARGERY WALKER	
		Miss MARJORIE WITHEY	

The action passes in a room in a pauper refuge of a mountain village in Germany
It is divided into two parts
The first part closes with the apparition of the three angels of light
Interval of Ten Minutes
The Second Part terminates with the death of Hannele
Costumes and properties manufactured by the Repertory Theatre Staff

Business Manager	Mr. THOMAS J. PIGOTT
Acting Manager	Mr. OSCAR WADDINGTON
Stage Manager	Mr. ARTHUR K. PHILLIPS
Assistant Stage Managers	Mr. RICHARD COKE and Mr. J. R. COLLINS

THE GAIETY is exceptionally well p... from FIRE by reason of ... HOFFMANN Sprinkler In... stallation, Hydrants, Hand Ex-tinguishers, and Drilled Staff. Moreover, in case or emer-gency, the Theatre can be EMPTIED IN LESS THAN TWO MINUTES

The Observer *found 'an excellent Slightly in Mr Noël Coward' and MacLiammóir (né Alfred Willmore) was to retain fond memories of being told the facts of life by Noël in a Glasgow dressing-room during the post-London tour.*

Centre: Gertrude Lawrence, as she was when Noël first met her on the train going up to rehearse Hannele at the Liverpool Rep in the spring of 1913: 'She wore a black satin coat and a black velvet military hat with a peak; her face was far from pretty but tremendously alive, she carried a handbag and a powder puff and frequently dabbed her generously turned-up nose . . . she gave me an orange and told me a few mildly dirty stories and I loved her from that moment onwards.'

The Light Blues: *a Cambridge musical comedy starring Albert Chevalier, Shaun Glenville, Jack Hulbert and his wife of a few weeks Cicely Courtneidge, who recalled later that Noël was 'a thin, pale-faced youth who always seemed to know everything and infuriated me because he was always right.'*

The Happy Family: *a bizarre piece during which the entire cast were turned into animals, barring Noël, who was thus left to sing a rousing military number entitled 'Sentry Go' in the second act. 'He combines', said the* Daily Telegraph, *'the grace of a Russian dancer with the manners of a public schoolboy.' Noël carried a fraying copy of the review around in his jacket pocket for several weeks.*

Their other close friend during these years was John Ekins, a handsome youth, every bit as stage-struck as Stodge and Podge, with already two good West End parts to his credit. 'The threesome became inseparable', Mrs Coward writes, 'they were always very happy together' and John would rush up from London to see the others when they were on tour. 'Esmé and I had a lovely time with John and we did enjoy Stratford awfully. We saw the Birthplace of the Immortal Bard!' They read quantities of poetry, the more romantic and passionate the better, and Noël and Esmé endeavoured to write poetry themselves. One thick notebook of Noël's survives, from which one can gather that he, from the first, inclined towards the funny – or at least attempted to be witty; Esmé inclined more towards the passionate and disillusioned. Noël copied one or two of Esmé's efforts into his notebook, either because he was trying to set them to music or because she had supplied him with lyrics at his request:

Lyric for Duet

Garth
Through the tumbled flowers of dead years
Through sudden music and most bitter pain
Leaving the memories of smiles and tears
Came this white love of mine to bloom again.

Lady Gay
One signs, one tells, that is all.
One buys, one sells, that is all.
So if this rose is canker'd at the heart
And if this song is hollow from the start
One sighs, but is wise, that is all.

Esmé Wynne

At the age of sixteen Noël wrote both the words and music of a song called *Forbidden Fruit*, the first song he considered to be 'whole and complete'; and that is how it remained until its publication, unaltered, thirty-seven years later. (Fifty-two years later it was sung by Daniel Massey as the youthful Noël in the film *Star*.) But it was a remarkable achievement for the adolescent composer, who always looked back with affectionate tolerance and amusement to the very first signs of the sophistication and cynicism for which he was to become so famous. Two years later we find him still trying to be 'naughty' and funny simultaneously:

Little French Lady

verse I
Once in a corner of England
There lived a good little maid
She soon grew horribly weary
Of being so prim and so staid.
And then there came to the village
A Frenchman dapper and gay,
He took her driving just once or twice
And smiled on hearing her say . . .

refrain
I'd like to be a little French lady
I'd like to live in a little French town
I'd like to have a lovely ring
And a beautiful evening gown
I'd like to have a little French sweetheart
And he must love me . . . night and day
And I would like to spend . . . a week end
In the sweet Parisienne's way!

verse 2   He found her manners delightful
           He found her kisses so sweet
           He said 'You're tout à fait charmante'
           And knelt at her tiny feet.
           She gazed at him in compassion
           And as the weather was hot
           She wasn't sure of the French for 'No'
           So had to say 'Oui' on the spot . . .

Then again there was the early attempt to be joky in this little number written when he was just eighteen:

I'm Not A Fool As A Rule

When I was a child
I drove my parents wild
I used to ask them questions all the day.
Father used to frown
And put his paper down
'The kid's a bally lunatic' he'd say.
Then Mother used to smile and cry 'The Darling,
He really has the most abnormal brain'.
But I'm never certain quite
As to which of them was right:
I've tried to make my mind up, but in vain . . .

Mother used to say that I was clever
Father always told me I was not
And between them both
I give my solemn oath
I knew not which was which or what was what.
How often I have tried to solve the puzzle
And sometimes I'm afraid I never will.
When I was quite a child I had the colic
And they said the thing to cure it was a pill
It's bad to hesitate
So I swallowed seven or eight.
I'm not a fool as a rule, but still . . .!

One year later, in 1919 as far as can be ascertained, the name Noël Coward appeared on the cover of a published song for the first time: *The Baseball Rag*, with, in bright red letters: 'Words by Noël Coward, Music by Doris Doris' (as his new collaborator Doris Joel preferred to be known).

One surprising fact emerges from Noël's bulging notebook: that at the immature age of eighteen, one of his very first attempts to write a three-act play should already have been on the subject of drugs. Surprising, because all his life Noël was to have a hatred, almost amounting to fear, of hallucinatory drugs, yet was eternally fascinated by them and the people who took them, and found them amusing subjects for his particular brand of comic dialogue. And this play – untitled and unfinished – is significant because his first great hit, *The Vortex*, written four or five years later, deals with the same subject. Note too his first use here of 'Elvira' as a Christian name. The curtain rises on act one of this untitled piece with everybody at the coffee stage of dinner, and Noël quickly takes the plunge:

IRIS:	Then you've been to China, Mr Saville?
KATT:	I've visited practically every interesting part of the world.
IRENE:	Have you been to Paris?
KATT:	Well yes, that is generally the first place to go.
IRENE:	I've never gone farther than Ryde. But still that's something.
LADY CARRINGTON:	Undoubtedly.
IRIS:	I like men who go about a bit and see life.
LADY C.:	I suppose that is why so many women marry commercial travellers.
ALICE:	But do go on telling us about the opium den, Mr Saville. It's frightfully thrilling.
KATT:	There's really nothing more to tell. The temporary satisfaction given by the drug doesn't last long, then one once more becomes normal and generally the victim of horrible depression.
ELVIRA:	But really it's worth it. Think how glorious it must be to merge one's personality into a fantastic world of sensuous dreams.
LADY C.:	Really, Miss Lestrange, some of your ideas verge on the indecent.
IRIS:	I rather agree with Elvira. It must be a wonderful sensation.
MAJOR C.:	Damned unhealthy form of amusement, I call it.
MRS H-N.:	One wouldn't expect a man like you to be in the least attracted to drug taking, dear Major. It appeals to the more degenerate natures.
NORMAN:	I should love to try it.
LADY C.:	My dear boy, your frantic efforts to be decadent are almost pathetic.
IRIS:	I should love to smoke just one little pipe of opium, just to see what happened.
KATT:	You'd probably be able to obtain the same result by crossing the Channel on a rough day.
IRENE:	Oh, how disgusting! But I'm really a splendid sailor.
MRS H-N.:	But I thought you said you'd never been farther than Ryde.
IRENE:	Those Solent boats rock dreadfully. Mother said it was splendid of me not to be ill.
LADY C.:	If there's one topic of conversation I thoroughly dislike, it's *mal de mer*. Couldn't we talk of something else?
EDWARD:	Democracy!
LADY C.:	That's equally nauseous but less blatant.
IRIS:	I'd prefer to continue our discussion of drugging.
KATT:	Doping is the correct term.
ELVIRA:	How *too* descriptive.
HILARY:	Doping is quite a hobby among society women in Paris.
JIMMY POOL:	By Jove, I'd like to see some of them at it!
IRIS:	I knew a girl who used to drug a lot. Her descriptions of the sensation were most interesting.
KATT:	What happened to her eventually?
IRIS:	She went into a convent and now spends her time in penitence and prayer.
LADY C.:	Praying only becomes really trying when one has linoleum in one's bedroom.
MRS H-N.:	Or furry rugs, they tickle one's knees.
MAJOR C.:	So reminiscent of picture palaces. (Laughs uproariously)
LADY C.:	Charlie, please remember that this is not the club.
MAJOR C.:	Sorry, my dear.
MRS H-N.:	Well, if a nunnery is the ultimate end of doping, I hope heaven will save me from it.
EDWARD:	I hope heaven will save you from it anyhow, Mrs Naigrill.

The Knight of the Burning Pestle, *and the start of the Betty Chester friendship: Noël played Ralph at Birmingham in 1919 and in the West End in 1920. 'There was', he said, 'a quality of fantasy about the whole engagement', one which involved hurling buns into Maud Gill's mouth while she was disguised as a bear. The Chester friendship came to an abrupt end when she refused to lend Noël £40, claiming that she had just been robbed. Noël checked with the local police station, found she hadn't and that was that.*

Ralph was delightfully handled by Mr. Noel Coward. There was no mistaking his vocation. He became the real fantastic knight of the flaming pestle, and his knight errantries were carried out with a glorious flourish of voice and posture. Mr. Halliwell Hobbes

TO DEAR MOTHER

Easter brings greetings
Easter brings love
Easter brings Happiness
From far above

From

Noël

NIGHTMARE AFTER CHRISTMAS DINNER

OHO-O-O !!!

VERY FRENCH

MADAME! EET-EES EXQUEESIT,
EES, EET NOT?

VERY GERMAN.
I HAF SOM SAURKRAUT

GOING COURTING

Noël Coward, boy artist: though he was never to carry on with the caricatures, he did return late in life to the easel and painting was to become the last great non-professional occupation of his fifties and sixties.

Opposite above: Pavlova and Nell Gwynn; below, a painting in the style of Edmond Dulac.

32

NELL GWYN

And much, much more on the same subject, until at the end of Act Three – according to Noël's synopsis – Edward has a furious row and then a passionate love scene with Iris, at the end of which he pulls himself together and persuades her to go back to her husband; he contemplates shooting himself but finally decides that turning it all into a best-seller would be more profitable.

Two other small but significant clues are apparent in this early effort: Noël's future love of travel and the fun to be extracted from it, which he later used in all his comedies, and his genius for the comic use of place names not funny in themselves, e.g. 'Ryde' in contrast to 'China'.

'I was so overpoweringly witty at the age of eighteen that I shudder to think of it,' Noël said in a speech he made nearly half a century later. So as to leave no literary stone unturned (and one can assume out of competition with Stoj), Poj also wrote two novels at this time which, he says, mercifully never saw the light. *Cats and Dogs*, the first, was about a vivacious brother and sister, an idea quite shamelessly stolen from Shaw's *You Never Can Tell*, and one which came in very handy three years later when he wrote a play called *The Young Idea*; by this time the brother and sister had become twins, making the resemblance to Shaw's play more marked than ever. The second novel was called *Cherry Pan*, after the daughter of the great god Pan, and was written during Stoj and Poj's romantic pagan period – both the nicknames and the novel later became embarrassing with the weight of years, though highly enjoyable at the time. Although this whimsical, half-fairytale source of inspiration flourished concurrently with Noël's sophisticated would-be cynicism, he seems to have succeeded in making the most of both and also 'living' the two sides of his character separately. During the romantic period, while he and Esmé were in Torquay with *Charley's Aunt*, he reports that they took advantage of the warm spring weather to 'frolic merrily in woodland glades fringing the shore and dance naked on hidden beaches'. Cherry Pan, in the novel, was a whimsical little beast who had materialized one summer evening in Sussex and then, scantily clad and garrulous to a degree, had raised all hell in the nearby rectory. Noël finally polished her off, rather lamely, by sending her back to where she came from in the first place – an elfin grotto, no less.

He gave novel writing a rest for the next eleven years, and then he half finished *Julian Kane*, a neurotic story about a young man who committed suicide because he was bored. This he showed to William Bolitho, tall, fair, blue-eyed and the distinguished author of *Twelve Against The Gods* and *Murder For Profit*. 'William said sharply, "Be careful about death. It's a serious business, big and important. You can't go sauntering towards death with a cigarette hanging from your mouth".' Twelve months later William 'set out quietly on his voyage through the dark fields of eternal silence' – he committed suicide. Noël, however, persevered with *Julian Kane* for a long time, until it occurred to him that future readers would find the reading of it as tedious as the writing of it had become to him: they too might die from boredom. He put it away for good and had to wait until 1960, when his only published novel, *Pomp and Circumstance,* enjoyed success in England and America.

All his life Noël seems to have been attracted, as though by destiny, towards those men and women who climbed to the pinnacles of fame and success in their chosen careers. And so it was in the summer of 1917, curious and rather wonderful to relate, that he should have made his first film appearance in *Hearts of The World* by David Wark Griffith, greatest of

Opposite: Noël's first attempt at painting in oils after Churchill had commanded him to give up watercolours.

directors. Mr Griffith was a pioneer, the first to realize the artistic potentialities of cinema, an experimenter with new techniques and the inventor of the close-up. Although *Hearts of The World* cannot justifiably be included among his masterpieces, he did for the first time include in the story actual scenes shot for the purpose at the Front during the First World War. Noël's appearance cannot be counted among his greatest either, consisting as it did of only a few days' work on location in Worcestershire, pushing a wheelbarrow in a supposedly French village street. With typical courage Noël 'helped' the great director to direct, pointing out to Mr Griffith that it would be more sensible for him to push the wheelbarrow towards, instead of away from, the camera. He also made friends with the stars of the film, Lillian and Dorothy Gish; his ties with Lillian remained strong till the end of his days. So many frames of his scene with Lillian were snipped away from the few rare copies that his appearance in the film today amounts to no more than a flash, but the 'still' of the extremely young Lillian and Noël has become one of the most familiar of all.

Noël's mother and her sister Vida were proud of their Scottish Lowland ancestry; their father, Captain Henry Veitch, Royal Navy, had for some years been British Consul in Madeira and one of his sisters had married into a titled Scottish family, the Haigs of Bemersyde. Aunt Vida in particular loved to gloat nostalgically over the family tree she had compiled with the help of Lord Lyon, King of Arms, but Noël would only feign an interest in all this to please her, not really caring about what little blue blood flowed in their veins, especially now that they were living in reduced circumstances in a maisonette in Clapham – 'genteel poverty' Noël called it. Mr Coward's job with Payne's pianos lingered on, continuing to dwindle until it evaporated entirely, from which time on he contented himself constructing model yachts and sailing them on the Clapham Common pond.

Mrs Coward (like her son, ever the one to take action in a hopeless situation) courageously took the lease, which included all the furniture, on a tall and far larger house at 111 Ebury Street and, ancestral glories for the time being brushed aside, decided to make a living taking in lodgers. A certain amount of grandeur compensated for the day-long drudgery she so bravely undertook, for a niece of Lord Brassey occupied the third-floor front; everyone, including the Coward family, dressed each night for dinner and the two maids changed into black with starched white caps and aprons.

Noël had a little room under the roof, which he enjoyed, and he much preferred living in Belgravia because of its proximity to the pleasures of the West End. But this happy state of affairs did not last for long as far as Mrs Coward was concerned: they soon found they had to make do with only one maid, which meant that she had to slave away at some of the housework as well as doing all the cooking and shopping economically. Anxiety hung like a pall over her until she had scraped together enough to pay the rates and the next quarterly instalment on the house. Even the great dread of those days – 'the broker's men' – appeared at the door as time went by, sternly demanding payment of bills long overdue until, she writes, she was at her wit's end. Noël, though still so young, was her one help morally and financially: 'He always knew the right thing to do, his opinion was law to me. When I was quite desperate at Ebury Street, he would talk and reassure me, go off and get money from somewhere and bring relief and joy to me.'

After six more worrying years Noël put an end to his mother's toil and fatigue by taking a cottage at Dockenfield in Surrey (which he could by then afford) and insisting, against all her arguments and protests, that she

The Saving Grace: *Noël played Ripley Guildford in this 1917 Charles Hawtrey–Gilbert Miller production with Mary Jerrold and Emily Brooke. 'I was so amazed to get a job in the all-star cast', wrote Noël later, 'that I shouldn't have turned half a hair if they'd told me Ellen Terry was to play my baby sister.'*

must have a long rest in the country air away from 'that beastly house', while his father must manage as best he could to run it. Mr Coward, who could exert just as much smiling charm as his son when he wanted to, unexpectedly made a great success of it, making jolly jokes with the lodgers and an ally out of May the housemaid, whom he let have her head to the undreamed-of extent of not wearing her starched cap *at all,* and singing or whistling, if she wished, all the livelong day.

The First World War had not made much of an impression on Noël, but now, in 1918 – his age the same as that of the century – he became due for call-up. He had already been medically examined and pronounced unfit for active service, but told to expect to be called upon for lighter duties in the Army. This he regarded as a tiresome, useless and unpleasant interruption of his career and of his avowed intention to become famous as soon as possible, and therefore rich enough to support his mother and himself in comfort. To be fair to Noël, everyone else was by now war-weary. After four years of blacked-out streets, casualty lists, coupons and food rationing, the glamour of war, of bravery and patriotism, had given way to a mood of cheerless resignation. The sinister call-up card fell through the

Left: Hearts of the World, *D. W. Griffith's film 'for the War effort' conceived in Holywood, set in France and shot largely in England. The stars were Lillian and Dorothy Gish, the former to become a lifelong friend, and Noël wrote: 'I was paid, I think, a pound a day for which I wheeled a wheelbarrow up and down a village street in Worcestershire. The film left little mark on me beyond a most unpleasant memory of getting up at five every morning and making my face bright yellow.' It was to be twenty years before he filmed again.*

Above: Maxine Elliott as Britannia in a charity matinée during the First World War. *Left:* Gaby Deslys: an early heroine of Noël's.

letter-box at Ebury Street one morning, an immediate death-knell to his happy optimism at having obtained a jolly good part at no less than fifteen pounds a week in a new play by Hazel May, already in rehearsal. He reported at once to Camberwell Baths, was marched to Whitehall with fifty others, and thence entrained to Hounslow, where next day they were decked out in ill-fitting khaki. He had been unable to let his mother know any of this and was in consequence wretched.

The keynote of Noël's nine months in the Artists Rifles is one of dismal unhappiness: 'one long exercise in futility' as he described it. According to his mother he was more trouble than he was worth, in and out of hospitals all the time, and he 'did not help the war along very much. Much to my astonishment he was given a pension for thirteen weeks and a medal when he was discharged!' There was no room in Noël's heart even for recognition of his poor showing as a soldier, only thankfulness that he was once more free to shape his life as he wanted.

Mrs Coward carefully saved every important scrap of memorabilia from Noël's birth to early manhood, with one marked exception – the War. Not one document survives, no discharge papers even, and not a single

Right: Ivor Novello, seven years older than Noël and, at the time of their first meeting, considerably more successful; 'Noël was infinitely more intelligent and more talented as an actor', wrote Esmé Wynne later, 'but Ivor was on first acquaintance much more affectionate and sweet.'

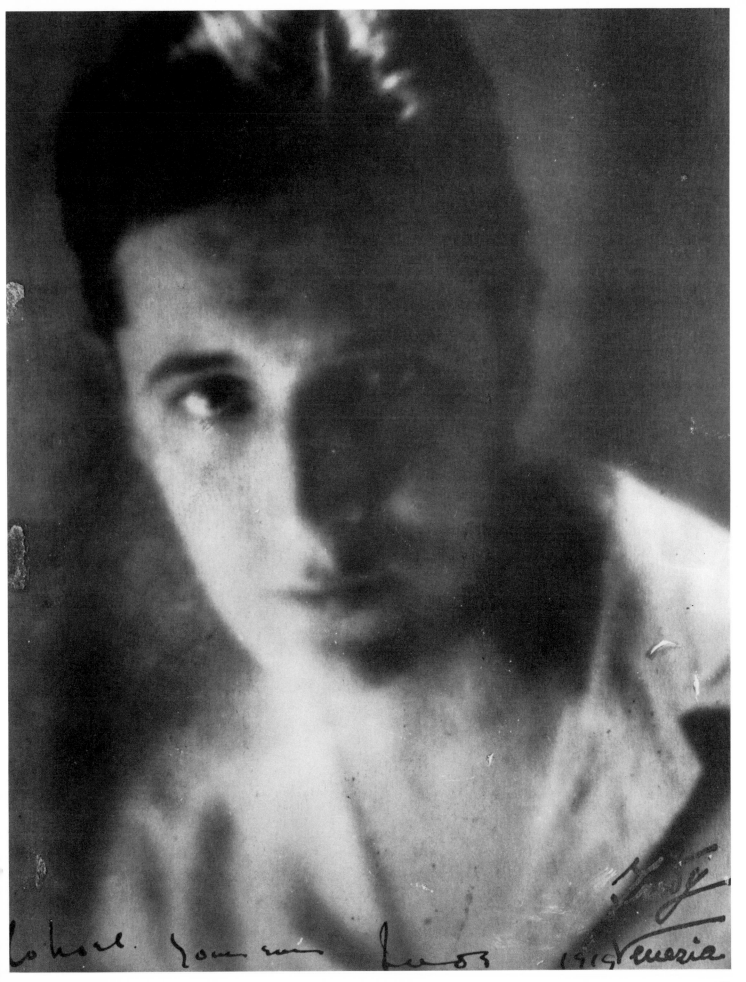

photograph of Noël in uniform for us to reproduce in this book. Perhaps he tore these up himself or burnt them.

Within a month of the Armistice Noël was in a play called *Scandal* at the Strand Theatre, which he enjoyed. Backstage he enjoyed himself too much, poking fun at the three old ladies in the cast until he went too far and was given the sack. There then followed months of unemployment, his mornings spent in making the dreary rounds of theatrical agent's offices, only to be met with 'Nothing for you today' or 'We'll let you know'. The humiliation of these rebuffs was made less dreadful, or rather was offset, by Noël now considering himself primarily a serious writer. Whimsy was banished: no elfin sprites or sensual fauns ever again materialized, their places taken by courtesans with painted faces, pimps, tarts and even adulterers. He worked hard and managed to sell some of his short stories, but the phase finally petered out because most magazine editors ignored the efforts he sent them or found them too lurid.

Here is Mrs Coward's valedictory to her son's youth:

Noël was now a tall, well set-up young man, very very popular. He was always witty and amusing, made wonderful friends who wanted him always with them. He was wrapped up in the theatre and everything connected with it, and, when people used to be so shocked to think he had had no real education, I always said and felt that he was having his education for his career. Noël learnt so much from Charles Hawtrey and where could he have found better training for his career than with Hawtrey? He was always so very much interested in Noël, appreciated his cleverness and humour and often repeated his remarks.

Mrs Coward ends her memoirs in May 1934 with:

Noel is writing such a terribly interesting book [*Present Indicative*] with a lot about his childhood days and our happy times together. So there is no need for me to tell more, but I thought I would put down something of his real babyhood, and anyhow it has passed a few happy hours for me, recalling the past.

MR. NOËL COWARD MAKING MENTAL NOTES
FOR THE FIRST PART OF "CAVALCADE."

2
THE
TWENTIES

NOËL COWARD IS FOR MANY PEOPLE THE EMBODIMENT OF THAT feverish era now known as the Twenties, and in the literary, theatrical and social histories of the time he was – and he remains – a lasting and significant figure. 'I was', he says, 'more intimately and turbulently connected with the British theatre than anyone else I can think of,' and, though thirteen months out of the ten years brought him three resounding and spectacular failures, for most of the remainder, 'success took me to her bosom like a maternal boa constrictor'.

1920, the first year of 'his' decade, was kind to him to begin with and gave him a fitting and auspicious welcome. In May, *I'll Leave It To You* was produced in Manchester with Noël in a leading role, to public and critical acclaim, repeated with the London production in July, when it had a roaringly successful first night with 'Young Playwright of Great Promise' notices the next morning. Yet it ran for just thirty-seven performances. The same thing happened all over again a year or so later with *The Young Idea*, which ran for sixty-seven. But no matter; the critics had hailed the new dramatist, describing him as 'an infant prodigy' and 'an amazing youth', and agreeing that for his age he showed 'astonishing' gifts and predicting for him a radiant future.

For years Noël had dreamed of this moment – waking up on the morning after a first night and eagerly opening the papers to find reviews as rapturously encouraging as even he could have hoped for. Disillusionment with the critics, of course, set in after both plays failed; but later on he maintained that these experiences had been very good for him. If the plays had failed despite good notices, there must be something wrong with them that had to be put right. What was it? His mind went back to the warning Gilbert Miller had given him a year or so ago: 'Your dangerous facility for writing clever dialogue, which you must guard against. A play must be as strongly constructed as the foundations of a house. Dialogue is the decoration.' All right, the next straight play he wrote must be 'stronger'. And so it was – the play was *The Vortex*. (Two of the three flops produced in 1926–7 had been written before this resolution 'to do better' and were consigned to limbo in a drawer from which they should never have emerged. Later still, Noël affirmed that these three calamities had also been salutary; he even maintained that he had been 'lucky' to have experienced and suffered from failure early, and to have discovered he had enough guts to overcome it.)

Noël's engagement in *Polly With A Past* in May 1921 is unremarkable except for three things: his over-acting badly while 'fighting like a steer' to get laughs from unfunny lines; his walks home from the theatre to Ebury Street with the young Edith Evans, during which they forecast with certainty their future stardom; and, after three months of *Polly,* his sudden, irresistible urge to go to America to see for himself New York and the million lights of Broadway. All obstacles, including the lack of money for a ticket, were surmounted and Noël sailed with Jeffery Holmesdale (now Earl Amherst), his 'ideal travelling companion', in the *Aquitania* in May. Too late – though, in fact, as early as the ship's leaving Cherbourg – he began to fear that he might have embarked on a rash, albeit exciting,

One idol with another.

adventure, and he was right: it proved to be both. All he had materially was a one-way ticket, seventeen pounds in cash, more than a few manuscripts which he hoped to sell and, fortunately, quite a smart wardrobe. Intangibly, he had his unquenchable belief in himself and his talents, and the hope that he might take Broadway by storm.

When visiting somewhere for the first time it is remarkable that, among all the good advice, one vital piece of information is withheld: no one ever tells you, for instance, that every metal doorknob in New York is capable of giving you an electric shock. In Noël's case what no one had told him was of far more importance – that nearly every theatre in New York City would be firmly closed from June until September. (In those days, before air-conditioning, the heat in a theatre with an audience would have been unbearable.) He, therefore, had little more than three weeks in which to present his letters of introduction and his scripts to the important managers, all of whom treated him kindly, told him they were getting out of town and that there would be nothing doing until the autumn. He had in the meantime learnt his way about the city, mastered the mysteries of the New York subway, and done as much theatre-going as he could afford. The much faster tempo of the acting compared to that in London electrified him and made a lasting impact on his own acting and the lightning-quick

World's Pictorial News

EXCLUSIVE NEWS, BEST PICTURES, THE WEEK'S SPORT, POWERFUL SERIALS, THEATRICAL NOTES, SOCIETY GOSSIP

No. 39.   Sent to any address in the British Isles, 2s. 2d. per quarter.   FRIDAY, JULY 30, 1920.   Registered at the G.P.O. as a Newspaper.   THREE HALFPENCE.

TRIUMPHS OF YOUTH ON STAGE AND SCREEN.

Wonderful Charm and Artistry of Edna Best.

Prophecy About an Actress That Came True.

IT is said of Noël Coward that, when he was very young and had been exceptionally naughty one day, his mother said to him: "Didn't you ask God yesterday to make you a better boy?" "Well, he hasn't done it, has he?" said young Noël, with bright and destructive logic.

It is this shrewd perception and fund of unexpected humour which, probably, accounts for this young actor-author's convincing success with his new play, "I'll Leave it to You," which began its merry career at the London New Theatre only a few evenings ago.

Mr. Noël Coward is not yet twenty-one, but already he has completed three other plays, with the

Noel Coward's Record for Three Plays.

Amazing Successes of Joan Morgan.

Miss Edna Best.

Noël Coward.

SAVOY THEATRE

Proprietors   THE SAVOY THEATRE LTD.
Licensed by the Lord Chamberlain to Mr. RUPERT D'OYLY CARTE, Savoy Hotel, W.C.
Lessees   The Executors of H. B. Irving.
Under the management of ROBERT COURTNEIDGE.

ROBERT COURTNEIDGE presents

NOEL COWARD   KATE CUTLER   ANN TREVOR

THE YOUNG IDEA

"Where shall we go to my pretty maid?"

NEW THEATRE
I'LL LEAVE IT TO YOU

"Sir, she said."

Modelled closely on Shaw's You Never Can Tell, *Noël's second London play (as author) was about a couple of precocious children who reunite their estranged parents. With a cast which also featured Kate Cutler, Austin Trevor, Herbert Marshall and Leslie Banks, The Young Idea ran all of seven weeks in the West End: 'Mr Coward', wrote St John Ervine for the* Observer, *'has not yet conquered his habit of writing plays as if they were charades.' The* World Pictorial News, *however, voted him that year's 'best-dressed young wit in London' when reporting the opening of* I'll Leave It To You.

Polly With A Past: *an American farce which came into the St James's on 2 March 1921 with an immensely starry cast. With Noël (by now getting £20 a week for what he regarded as a thoroughly unrewarding 'feed' part) were two subsequent Hollywood officer-and-gentleman stalwarts, Claude Rains and C. Aubrey Smith, as well as Edna Best, Henry Kendall and a young Edith Evans, with whom Noël was not to work again until she starred in his National Theatre revival of* Hay Fever *forty years later.*

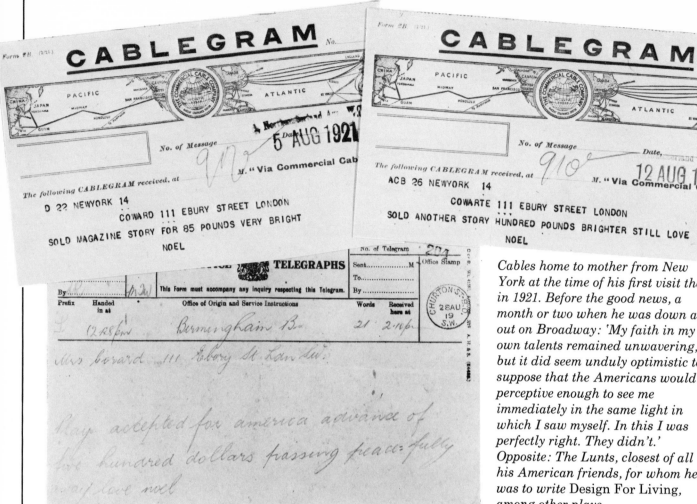

CABLEGRAM No.

Form #B (2/21.)

PACIFIC   ATLANTIC

No. of Message   5 AUG 1921

M. "Via Commercial Cab

The following CABLEGRAM received, at

D 22 NEWYORK 14

COWARD 111 EBURY STREET LONDON

SOLD MAGAZINE STORY FOR 85 POUNDS VERY BRIGHT

NOEL

CABLEGRAM No.

Form #B (2/21.)

CHINA   PACIFIC   ATLANTIC   ENGLAND
JAPAN   AFRICA

No. of Message   910   Date,

12 AUG 1921

M. "Via Commercial Cables,"

The following CABLEGRAM received, at

ACB 26 NEWYORK 14

COWARTE 111 EBURY STREET LONDON

SOLD ANOTHER STORY HUNDRED POUNDS BRIGHTER STILL LOVE

NOEL

TELEGRAPHS   No. of Telegram   204   Office Stamp

This Form must accompany any inquiry respecting this Telegram.

By   M 2v

Prefix   Handed in at   Office of Origin and Service Instructions   Words   Received here at

L   12.48pm   Birmingham B.   21   2.16pm

Mrs Coward 111 Ebury St Lon Sw.

Play accepted for america advance of
five hundred dollars passing peace-fully
.... love noel

Cables home to mother from New York at the time of his first visit there in 1921. Before the good news, a month or two when he was down and out on Broadway: 'My faith in my own talents remained unwavering, but it did seem unduly optimistic to suppose that the Americans would be perceptive enough to see me immediately in the same light in which I saw myself. In this I was perfectly right. They didn't.' Opposite: The Lunts, closest of all his American friends, for whom he was to write Design For Living, *among other plays.*

delivery of his comedy songs, at which he was to become unrivalled.

He now had three months in which to kick his heels. Money ran out and he moved to smaller and smaller rooms, until he was under the very eaves of the Brevoort Hotel, from which eyrie he was rescued by Gabrielle Enthoven and Cecile Sartoris, who gave him a room in their studio in Washington Square. Far from well-off themselves, they said he could pay the rent when he sold a play; then in August even they fled town to escape the heat, leaving Noël in the flat. Now he really was on his own; sometimes almost penniless, sometimes hungry, often lonely.

With the end of summer, Broadway awoke to activity; new plays were rehearsed and opened (some of them quickly closed, as usual), and with the return of all the managers came the return of all Noël's manuscripts. He re-read them with pleasure, thought the managers remarkably lacking in perspicacity, and was eventually able to make some money by turning *I'll Leave It To You* and *The Young Idea* into short stories for five hundred dollars each. Affluence! He moved back to the Brevoort (where Lester Donahue had a piano on which Noël could compose), he paid the kind Italian grocer who had allowed him credit for bacon and Chianti sparingly consumed over the months, and sent his mother forty pounds to make up for the loss of a lodger who had exchanged her first floor room in Ebury Street for the grave.

The friends Noël had made also came back to the city, the list headed by Lynn Fontanne and Alfred Lunt, who were, let us say, courting at the time and lived in Doctor Rounds' cosy theatrical digs in the West Seventies,

Baseball Rag

Verse I

I've got a ripping new sensation
There's just no need for hesitation
Baseball's the game that
makes the world go round
It gets your heart a palpitating
You can't sit still
you'll go mad you'll go mad
Because you'll never be
contented until.

Refrain

You do that Raggy Rag
Its just a Baseball time
And it gets you so syncopated mad
Like any old coon
You simply glide along dear
You never want to lag
Its —such its a[?] ... tally ho
For that Baseball Rag

where the food was good and Noël welcome to share it. It was here over supper, late into the night, that their friendship was forever cemented and their plans laid. First, however much Alfred's mother disliked her, Lynn would marry him; then they would all three become stars of international but equal magnitude and, to crown all, Noël (also world-renowned as a playwright) would write the perfect play for the three of them in which they would scintillate together on Broadway. The supper they had had on this particular night was potato salad and dill pickles. Noël says they became so over-excited by these optimistic orgies that they often had to walk to the corner and back to calm down, and once 'Lynnie and I sank so low that we made a charabanc trip to Chinatown'. But their dream did come true, in every particular, twelve years later with *Design For Living*.

Noël still had some bad patches to survive, borrowing money from Lynn and beginning to feel painfully homesick but with no means or hope of buying a ticket for England. Then, suddenly, there was a very small bout of moneymaking and Gladys Barber, a social Easthampton friend who had always been kind to Noël, persuaded her shipping-magnate husband to allow him a free passage in one of his ships – or so she told Noël. But did she, he often wondered, out of her generous heart pay for the passage herself?

He sailed in the S.S. *Cedric* on 31 October 1921. She was an old ship and very slow, which gave Noël pause to reflect on many things. He hadn't achieved much financially, only seven pounds more than he had left with, and had had no success whatever as an actor or a playwright. As a person,

The first published song, 1919. 'Doris Doris' was in reality Doris Joel, with whom he wrote a number of (largely unpublished) songs at this time; Baseball Rag *was, he regretted later, 'something less than all-American'.*

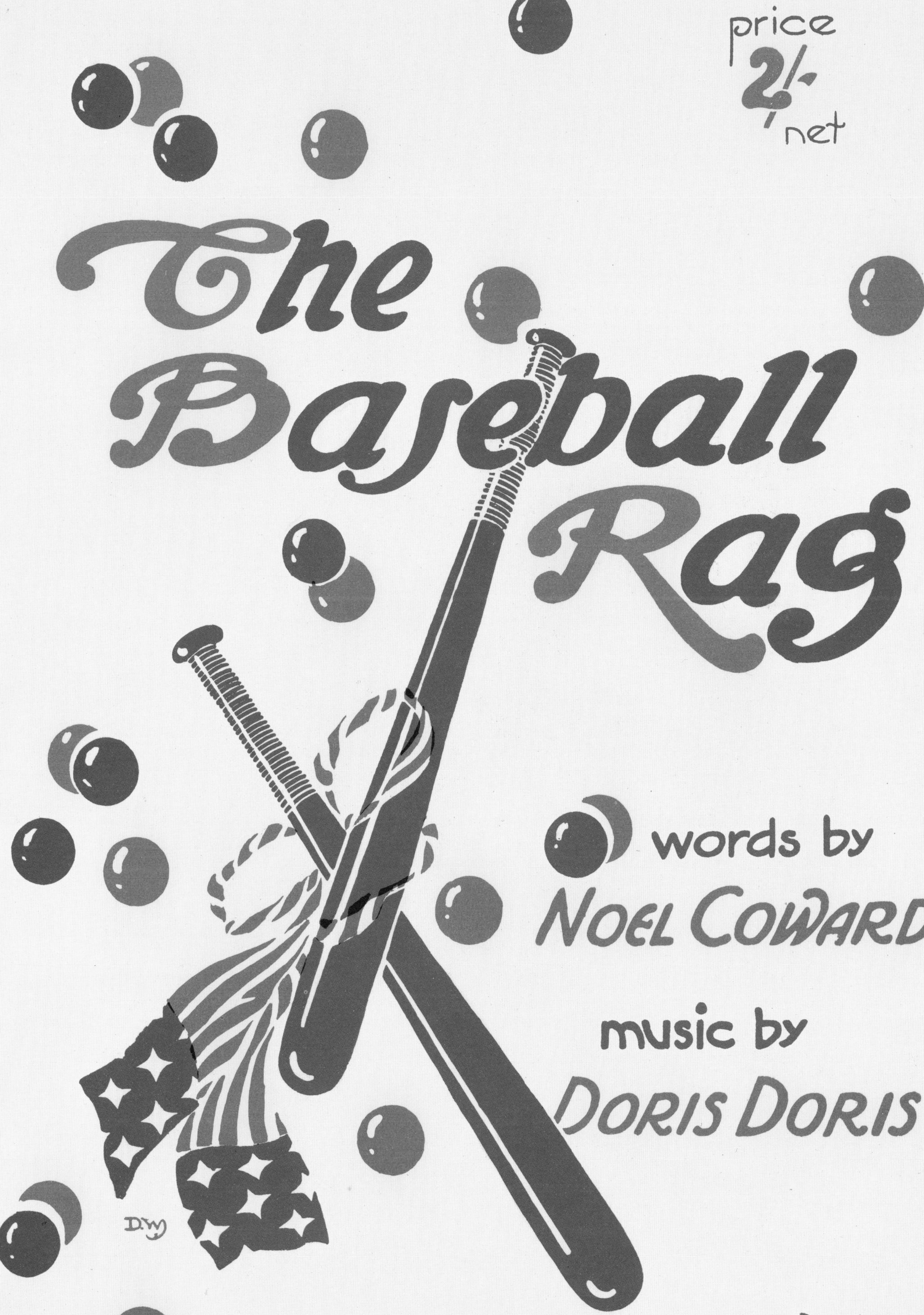

ASCHERBERG HOPWOOD & CREW Ltd
16 MORTIMER St LONDON W.1.
New York: LEO. FEIST (Inc.)

Noël experienced mixed pain and pleasure at seeing Jack Buchanan bring down the house in Charlot's Revue on Broadway – his own performance of his own songs in the London production had been less enthusiastically received.

Bea Lillie, an early and lifelong friend despite a series of major and minor quarrels along the way. At the end of their careers she played the lead in a musical version of his Blithe Spirit: 'as much like Madame Arcati', wrote Noël, 'as I am like Queen Victoria'.

In and out of costume with his lifelong friend and designer, Gladys Calthrop
(1924).

yes: towards the end of the six months he had been in demand socially, Lester Donahue had helped to open many closed doors, as had Lynn and Alfred, Laurette Taylor and Fred and Adele Astaire theatrically. He looked back and saw himself impeccably clad in white tie and tails, a popular figure at the very smartest first nights and without a nickel in his pocket to pay the subway home. But already distance was beginning to cast a romantic veil over the times of near-despair; he saw the sad yet gallant youth who had so courageously faced loneliness and sometimes hunger. Times hadn't been so bad after all. He remembered with affection all the friends he had made and would be enchanted to see again, and the kind Italian grocer, and the friendly neighbourhood cop who had lent him a gun because he'd worried about him being alone at night. He couldn't know that he would never see that side of life again, but, whatever happened, he had fallen in love with New York City for ever.

Lorn Loraine first came into Noël's life quite a while before this, at Betty Chester's parents' house in Chester Square. Betty took her stage name from the square (her real name was Grundtvig) and by 1921 was starring in *The Co-Optimists* and giving rather rowdy – known at the time as 'Bohemian' – after-the-theatre parties, by which late hour Mr and Mrs Grundtvig had retired respectably to bed. To everyone's surprise – including her own – Lornie too was 'on the stage', in the chorus of the hit musical *Irene* at the Empire, and was therefore quite at home in the atmosphere of Betty's parties, gay with exciting young guests – Gertie, Noël, Meggie Albanesi and Phyllis Monkman among them – dancing to the music of the wind-up gramophone. In this glamorous throng Lornie and Noël seem to have been irresistibly drawn to one another, though Noël describes her appearance as unremarkable and her figure 'unvoluptuous'. But, somehow, the unlikely friendship flourished and worked unfailingly well for the next forty-six years, until Lornie's death. She was tallish and fair, with an air of distinction and quiet authority allied to a bawdy sense of humour, her ribald remarks uttered in a well-bred voice; it was this unusual combination of qualities which attracted Noël to her in the first place.

Her closest friend was Meggie Albanesi, the gifted young actress who was as much loved by the public as by the critics, the latter prophesying that she would become the greatest actress of her time. And so, when *Irene* ended, Lornie, in need of a living, went to help with Meggie's fan mail and to work as part-time secretary to her mother, E. Maria Albanesi, one of the most popular novelists of the day. Noël had, meanwhile, moved down from his attic in Ebury Street to a more impressive room on the floor below in which he gave tea parties less rowdy than Betty's, as his father had to bring in the teatray and do the honours, but the guest list was more or less the same. Lornie was always there; and, after Meggie's early death, for Lornie to go to work full time for Noël was the most natural and easy move. Noël came to rely on her commonsense, good advice and gaiety in the years to come and wrote that she 'has been one of the mainstays of my life and one of the most truly important characters in it'.

Lord Lathom was young, very rich, tubercular, and his many friends called him Ned. Tuberculosis was in those days incurable; his doctors ordered him to Davos in Switzerland for its alleviation, and his friends rallied round in a successful attempt to give him a happy 1922 Christmas. He had already bought two of Noël's songs out of kindness at a time when Noël badly needed the money, and Noël was the first to arrive at Davos (his introduction to winter sports and their accompanying pleasures) to help Ned buy expensive presents for the others, and more baubles with which to deck the Christmas tree. Gladys Cooper, dazzling, was among the guests, and so was Edward Molyneux, the gifted young dress designer, and the popular Mrs Teddie Thompson. From America came Clifton Webb – already a singing and dancing star on Broadway – and Elsa Maxwell with her genius for party-giving and party-going. What more natural than for Noël to entertain this all-star cast with his songs at the piano in the evenings, and for Ned to declare that, with the songs he had already bought, there was almost enough material for an entire revue, and to telegraph to André Charlot to come out to Davos at once? Charlot, as famous at that time as Cochran for his smart and witty revues, came at once and Noël wrote to his mother: 'I am to do all the music for the new Charlot revue . . . and also all the words – isn't it thrilling? It will probably open in March at the Prince of Wales's with Maisie Gay and Gertrude Lawrence! I've just played all the music to Charlot and he's *delighted* – he sat without a smile, then took me aside and said that they were *all* good – so that's that – I now quite definitely enter the ranks of British Composers!' And what more natural, too, than for Molyneux to design the clothes for the revue, bearing his indefinable stamp and looking as chic in the photographs today as they were in 1923.

London Calling marked the first adult partnership of Noël Coward and Gertrude Lawrence, an association unmatched for glamour during their lifetimes and a legend to this day. Apart, they were tall, elegantly slim and chic, and so well groomed that they shone. Together they made magic; they both moved beautifully, could dance and 'put over' a number inimitably, played comedy with brilliance and, when called upon in a tender love scene, could move you to tears.

MR. NOEL COWARD
Who is part author and also acts—**and** dances—very well in "London Calling"

Gertie had graduated from the chorus in earlier Charlot Revues to playing small parts and understudying Beatrice Lillie; she'd married the stage manager, borne him a daughter, and left him. Noël put it this way: 'She married in haste and repented at Brixton.'

'Noël and Gertie' as an equally matched entity did not reach perfection until *Private Lives*; in fact, Noël provided Gertie with much better material in *London Calling* than he did for himself. She made a huge success with the haunting *Parisian Pierrot*, while he struggled in top-hat, white tie and tails with a song called *Sentiment*, but in vain. Not even the dance arranged and 'sweated over' by his friend Fred Astaire could save it. He exited night after night to lukewarm applause and it wasn't until he watched the nonchalant Jack Buchanan, months later in New York, easily stop the show with the same number that he realized he had been trying far too hard. 'This', he said, 'taught me a sharp lesson.'

He also supplied Maisie Gay with two hilarious numbers! *There's Life In The Old Girl Yet*, which she sang as a buxom but wilting soubrette with a large brooch flashing 'Baby' in diamanté from her bosom; and *The Swiss Family Whittlebot*, a parody of the Sitwells' 'modern' poetry. The latter resulted in a forty-year feud with the three Sitwells and earned several pages in the literary history of this century. Audiences, of course, loved it; Maisie as Hernia Whittlebot was dressed in shapeless sacking with large bunches of green grapes hanging from her ears and waist as she recited,

> Beloved, it is Dawn, I rise
> To smell the roses sweet
> Emphatic are my hips and thighs
> Phlegmatic are my feet

while her brother Gob, in cycling knickers and a velvet jacket, accompanied her with belch-like sounds and other rude noises issuing from a very peculiar musical instrument called the cophutican. The feud eventually ended with an affectionate reunion between Dame Edith and Noël, but from *London Calling* onwards 'modern' poetry became for him a source of prolonged hilarity and fitful irritation. He wrote and published two slim volumes of verse satirizing the real thing, but sometimes almost indistinguishable from it: *Chelsea Buns* 'by Hernia Whittlebot, edited by Noël Coward' and *Spangled Unicorn*, both of which have become collector's items.

He also let his gift for satire have its head with *A Withered Nosegay*, published in America as *Terribly Intimate Portraits*. Lornie helped him concoct this and contributed the illustrations, pen drawings of the subjects of the ten potted biographies, purporting to be 'after' Old Masters, or 'from a very old Russian oleograph' and so on. Among the subjects were the Eighth Duchess of Wapping (Madcap Moll), Donna Isabella Angelica Y Bananas, Maggie McWhistle, Bianca Pianno-Forti, and brave and witty Hortense Poissons, who was known as La Bibi, her life a rose-coloured smear across the history of France. Then there was Julie, Vicomtesse de Poopinac, who got herself to Versailles where she attracted the attention of the King by bumping into his arched back in the park (Dubarry had gone ahead, while he stooped to tie up his bootlace). She was soon installed in sumptuous apartments, her bedroom lined with costly brown and black tapestries picked out with beads and tufts of gloriously coloured wool. It was in her bed with curtains of a soft Norwegian yellow and massive tassels of crab mauve that she wrote most of the poems by which she is remembered, together with *The Pig-Sty*, a biting satire on life at Court. The press notices for *A Withered Nosegay* were almost unanimously enthusiastic: *Boxing Weekly* thought it 'Damn good', Auntie

Above and right: Gertrude Lawrence in the first of many roles created for her by Noël. 'Early Mourning' (London Calling, 1923) was an acid little sketch about a society lady being awakened to hear that her husband had just jumped off Waterloo Bridge and then discovering, to her subsequent rage, that the message was meant for somebody else. 'Tamarisk Town' and 'Parisian Pierrot' were just two of more than thirty production numbers in London Calling *(the title was an early 1923 acknowledgement of the BBC), first of the great Coward revues and the show that caused the Sitwell's vendetta with him – Edith seeing herself all too clearly in Hernia Whittlebot.*

THE SKETCH

REGISTERED AS A NEWSPAPER FOR TRANSMISSION IN THE UNITED KINGDOM AND TO CANADA AND NEWFOUNDLAND BY MAGAZINE POST.

No. 1599 — Vol. CXXIII.   WEDNESDAY, SEPTEMBER 19, 1923.   ONE SHILLING.

The poor typist day-dreams of the figure she will cut " when her ship comes home."

Hilda in *Fireside Fun* said 'Darling Chicks, get your Mumsie to buy it for your birthday', *The Playing Field* said 'Chaps! Buy this book!', *Capital and Labour* hoped it would not fall into the wrong hands, and all Herr von Grob could say in *The Austrian Tyrol* was 'Gott in Himmel'.

Reams have been written, at the time and ever since, about the first night of *The Vortex* on 16 December 1924, Noël's twenty-fifth birthday. Even the coconut matting on the floor of the Everyman Theatre (a converted drill-hall in Hampstead) got a mention: it couldn't be seen because of the fashionable crush. Lady Louis Mountbatten, Michael Arlen – with Noël, the other symbol of the Twenties – and Sir Edward Marsh, a first-nighter so famous he has to be described as 'inveterate', were among those present. Noël's first nights had already attained a fever-pitch of excitement they were never to lose. Celebrities predominated: film and stage stars, usually one or two members of the Royal family, and socialites galore with their concomitant Rolls Royces, furs and jewels. They were beginning to talk a language of their own: St John Ervine had already complained at having to sit next to a litter of them with their 'too divine' and 'simply marvellous darlings'. Whether the bright young things were trying to copy Noël's characters, who Mrs Patrick Campbell said 'talked like typewriting', or whether Noël was holding up the mirror to the socialites is not easy to decide, but one may suspect that it was the former.

The play caused a sensation from the first. That Noël was having trouble with the Lord Chamberlain over its 'unpleasant' theme had been common gossip in the West End for some time, which only added fuel to the titillation. It was all too true, but Noël had other problems to overcome, the scenery for a start. Gladys Calthrop, who had been associated with the play since its inception, was designing the clothes and sets for Noël for the first time (but far from the last – she designed them for all his plays for the next thirty years) and, owing to Norman Macdermott's having torn a fireplace out of one of her sets, she was out in the street until the last minute painting scenery propped up on the pavement. It was cold and very foggy, but fortunately for Gladys it didn't rain.

While she was thus occupied, Noël, with all his first-night anxieties only a few hours away, was in St James's Palace trying to convince Lord Cromer that, far from being immoral, his play was in fact the opposite: a moral tract castigating the *mores* of modern society. In this he succeeded and a licence was granted in the nick of time – he and Lord Cromer had had 'a spirited duel', he wrote. His major trouble, though, had taken place seven days before. Kate Cutler, a most accomplished and popular comedienne, one for whom Noël had especially written the part of the mother, unexpectedly and adamantly refused to go on with it. In this she was extremely foolish: Lilian Braithwaite, hitherto celebrated for her witty playing of gentle drawing-room comedies, took over the flamboyant and neurotic leading role and made the hit of her life.

And so the curtain went up in an electric atmosphere, with everybody's nerves (backstage and in front) taut and on edge. The applause at the end was no more terrific than it had been for Noël's two previous plays, but somehow he and Lilian knew that, when she asked, 'Do you think we're all right?', the question was merely rhetorical. They were more than all right – they and the play had been a triumph. Most of the papers next morning confirmed this, and agreed that Noël, after his showing in *London Calling*, was on the way to becoming what he was to remain for the rest of his life: the most versatile man in the modern British theatre. There were some dissident voices among the reviews, because of the play's 'shocking' degeneracy, which were of great help to the box office, and among the flood of letters Noël received there were several threats from apoplectic gentlemen to come and horsewhip him for his decadence. James Agate wrote what amounted to a eulogy, but among his four small criticisms was 'ladies do not exhale cigarette smoke through the nose'. When the play repeated its success in America, Mr Erlanger, the producer, refused to let his name appear on the playbills, because he was ashamed of the third act; it was, he said, a refutation of all that was meant by that sacred American institution, mother love.

The Vortex played to full houses in London for a year. Apart from having to give eight performances a week in that exacting leading part, the amount of sheer hard work and energy Noël put into it during those twelve months was astonishing. And with success came fame and fortune and their attendant trappings: he left his little attic room and took over the entire first floor in Ebury Street as his suite, which Gladys decorated in colours until then mainly associated with the Russian Ballet – clear bright scarlet clashing with shocking pink (known in those days as cerise) – and she also painted two murals of nudes over the fireplace. Noël, as will have been gathered, was fond of vivid colours, and ordered silk pyjamas and dressing-gowns in them by the half-dozen. In these exotic surroundings the more soberly dressed Lornie appeared each morning with a stack of mail to be dealt with, and on one occasion a press photographer was rashly allowed in to take a picture of Noël sitting up in bed. The flash resulted in Noël's half-closed eyes resembling those of a dope fiend in the last stages of addiction, and convinced outraged colonels and old fogies in general – curiously mostly male – more than ever of his depravity.

But hard work started quite soon on the new revue *On With The Dance*, with which Cochran would overtake André Charlot in expensive magnificence. Mr Cochran made it quite clear from the start of this, his and Noël's first association, that he did not consider Noël's music and lyrics

strong enough, and insisted that Noël confine himself to writing the sketches. Ideas for these came to Noël in quick abundance but, oddly enough, most of them led into an accompanying song and dance, so that when the revue was assembled it was found to everybody's surprise except Noël's that, with the exception of three songs by Philip Braham (with lyrics by Noël) and of the classical music for the ballets by Massine, all the score, book and lyrics were by Noël. His biggest and most enduring success from the show is *Poor Little Rich Girl*, which Cochran thought 'too dreary' and wanted to cut, but the dynamic star, Alice Delysia, who sang it, knew better. She suffered from an effective malady, when thwarted, of losing her voice so completely that she was forced to retire to her dressing-room and lock the door, sometimes for hours on end, while rehearsals came to a standstill. The illness lasted until she got her own way, when her voice fortunately came back to her. The poor little rich girl was played by Hermione Baddeley:

You're only a baby
You're lonely and maybe
Someday soon you'll know
The tears you are tasting
Are years you are wasting
Life's a bitter foe.
With fate it's no use competing
Youth is so terribly fleeting
By dancing much faster
You're chancing disaster
Time alone will show ...

Noël wrote many songs in the same vein of youthful disillusion during the Twenties, and this, with *Parisian Pierrot* before it, remains everlastingly popular as does one other yet to come (in 1928), *Dance Little Lady*:

Though you're only seventeen
Far too much of life you've seen
Syncopated child ...

One wonders today to what extent girls of seventeen had seen 'far too much of life' in the jazz-mad Twenties. Can it be that they really went all the way? Or were their elders sufficiently shocked by their appearance and behaviour? Hair Eton-cropped or shingled, scarlet lips, skirts above the knee, cigarettes in their long holders and sipping a Bronx cocktail – and then only going as far as flirting, necking and petting? So many of Noël's songs, funny and serious, had a peculiarly prophetic quality (*There Are Bad Times Just Around The Corner* and *Don't Let's Be Beastly To The Germans*) that one wonders whether these Twenties' 'world weary' lyrics have a truth that makes their appeal as strong as ever today. Or is it their enchantingly pretty, haunting melodies? Or is it the perfect marriage of the two that accounts for their imperishability?

Now it was Cochran's turn to be accused of decadence, that important ingredient of success at the box office. The *Morning Post* critic wrote: 'Mr Charles Cochran's new revue is at once the most decadent and most brilliant thing he has ever done. The whole thing is more than modern, bizarre, grotesque, fantastic, unnatural. The speed of the change from scene to scene, of the performance of each number is feverish, burlesquing the speed of our overheated life. At times the players seem mad, intoxicated. ...'

In the five months since *The Vortex* opened, Noël had acted in it, written,

THE VORTEX

A Play in Three Acts

by

NOEL COWARD.

Characters in order of their appearance:

Preston	- - -	CLAIRE KEEP
Helen Saville	- - -	MARY ROBSON
Pauncefort Quentin	- -	F. KINSEY PEILE
Clara Hibbert	- -	MILLIE SIM
Florence Lancaster	- -	LILIAN BRAITHWAITE
Tom Veryan	- - -	ALAN HOLLIS
Nicky Lancaster	- -	NOEL COWARD
David Lancaster	- -	BROMLEY DAVENPORT
Bunty Mainwaring	- -	MOLLY KERR
Bruce Fairlight	- -	IVOR BARNARD

THE PLAY REHEARSED BY THE AUTHOR
UNDER THE GENERAL DIRECTION OF
NORMAN MACDERMOTT.

ROYALTY THEATRE

Licensed by the Lord Chamberlain to DENNIS EADIE

Tuesday, December 16th, 1924, at 8.40

By arrangement with DENNIS EADIE
AND IN CONJUNCTION WITH
ALBAN B. LIMPUS and CHARLES KENYON
NORMAN MACDERMOTT
PRESENTS
THE EVERYMAN THEATRE COMPANY IN

THE VORTEX

A Play in Three Acts
By NOEL COWARD

Characters in the order of their appearance:

Preston	- - - -	KATHLEEN BLAKE
Helen Saville	- - -	MARY ROBSON
Pauncefort Quentin	- -	F. KINSEY PEILE
Clara Hibbert	- - -	MILLIE SIM
Florence Lancaster	- -	LILIAN BRAITHWAITE
Tom Veryan	- -	ALAN HOLLIS
Nicky Lancaster	-	NOEL COWARD
David Lancaster		BROMLEY DAVENPORT
Bunty Mainwaring	-	MOLLY KERR
Bruce Fairlight	-	IVOR BARNARD

THE PLAY REHEARSED BY THE AUTHOR
under the general direction of
NORMAN MACDERMOTT

'The Vortex was an immediate success and established me both as a playwright and as an actor, which was very fortunate, because until then I had not proved myself to be so hot in either capacity.'

The Sketch

REGISTERED AS A NEWSPAPER FOR TRANSMISSION IN THE UNITED KINGDOM AND TO CANADA AND NEWFOUNDLAND BY MAGAZINE POST.

No. 1683 — Vol. CXXX.　　　WEDNESDAY, APRIL 29, 1925.　　　ONE SHILLING.

NOEL THE FORTUNATE: THE YOUNG PLAYWRIGHT, ACTOR, AND COMPOSER, MR. NOEL COWARD,
BUSY AT BREAKFAST.

VOCAL FOX-TROT
First Love
FROM
CHARLES B. COCHRAN'S LONDON PAVILION REVUE
"ON WITH THE DANCE!"

WORDS & MUSIC BY
Noel Coward

Price 2/- Net

Ascherberg, Hopwood
& Crew, Ltd.
16, Mortimer St, London, W.1.

Left: 'The fault, dear Noël,' wrote Hannen Swaffer (never an admirer), 'lies not in our Mas [mothers] but in ourselves that we are slaves to drugs.' The Vortex publicity, replied Noël, 'though very good for business, became irritating after a while, and for years I was seldom mentioned in the press without allusions to cocktails, decadence and post-war hysteria.'

Alice Delysia was an enormous success in On With The Dance *singing* Poor Little Rich Girl *to Hermione Baddeley.*

composed and rehearsed for the Cochran revue, and had supervised a play he had written in 1923, *Fallen Angels*, which opened at the Globe only nine nights before *On With The Dance* at the Pavilion. He seems to have thrived on these tremendous and coincidental outbursts of energy, and to have on the whole enjoyed all the excitements and dramas brought about by three such varied entertainments. *Fallen Angels* was no exception: late in the day Margaret Bannerman, who was to have starred in it with Edna Best, collapsed and could not continue, whereupon Tallulah Bankhead rocketed in to the rescue. Tallulah – herself not disassociated in the public mind with sexy decadence – was at the apex of her notoriety with an army of fans, and her last-minute rescue work was a godsend to the gossip columns. She also happened to be a very good actress and on the opening night gave a dazzling performance of rocklike confidence in spite of only four days' rehearsal. She and Edna Best were called upon to play two chic, beautiful, young married women who get drunk over dinner while waiting for the arrival of their attractive French lover. They have both had affairs with him – before their marriages and not simultaneously, it must hastily be added. The uproar caused by so 'daring' a plot today seems unbelievable: obscene, shocking, vulgar, disgusting, nauseating and vile were among the abusive adjectives bandied about. It was not the sex angle so much as the sight of two well-bred young ladies getting progressively drunker and funnier all through the second act that caused the offense. Even as late as the last performance, when the curtain came down on this second act, a Mrs Hornibrook – the Mrs Whitehouse of her day – stood up in her box to make a public protest, but the orchestra struck up *I Want To Be Happy* and drowned her out.

Noël at this point had three successes running in the West End at the same time, and they were soon to be joined by another: the scripts nobody had thought good enough when he was in New York and ever since his return to London were in sudden demand – everything he had touched turned to gold. He had written *Hay Fever* for Marie Tempest, who hadn't cared for it, but a year and two flops later her manager came to Noël and said, 'I think she will like it now', and sure enough she did. Every actor and actress in London came to the last dress rehearsal and fell about with laughter, but thought the play too full of theatre 'shop' to be a success with the public. And Noël always recalled Eddie Marsh, that Dean of First-Nighters, giving him a sweet but pitying smile and saying, 'Not this time, Noël dear. Not this time.' After the dustbin filth accusations of the last few months, Noël had a lovely time with his first night speech – 'Whatever else you may think about the play, you must admit it's as clean as a whistle', but James Agate would have none of this. 'There is neither health

'Mr Coward', wrote the Sunday Times *of Fallen Angels, 'is a very young playwright of quite extraordinary gifts, who at the moment can no more be trusted with his talent than a schoolboy can be trusted who has stolen a piece of chalk and encountered a providentially blank wall.' Since its first production in 1925 the play has provided a vehicle for, among others, Edna Best, Tallulah Bankhead, Hermione Baddeley, Hermione Gingold, Nancy Walker, Dorothy Lamour, Joan Greenwood and Constance Cummings.*

nor cleanness about any of Mr Coward's characters, who are still the same vicious babies sprawling upon the floor of their unwholesome crèche.' The other critics gave the play very good notices but seemed determined to accuse Noël of something, and for the first time came the epithets which were to recur for many years – trivial, thin, flippant and brittle. Actually the play's construction is as strong as steel, strong enough to have lasted half a century and be given the status of a classic.

By the end of these twelve months of cloudburst successes and newspaper headlines, Noël had become the most talked-about young man in the country with full-page photographs in all the illustrated weeklies and every gossip-columnist straining to give examples of his nimble wit even, he maintained, if all he'd actually said was 'Pass the mustard'. The tumult and the shouting preceded him to America that autumn, where he was to repeat his triumph in *The Vortex* with the New York press agog that the miracle boy would also present no less than three other plays in the same season: *Hay Fever, Easy Virtue* and *The Queen Was In The Parlour*. And that was not all:

Whatever may be the portion of the impending Coward plays, it is safe to rely on the success of his new songs in the Charlot revue, which will bring Beatrice Lillie, Jack Buchanan and Gertrude Lawrence back to Broadway in October. He has dashed off two new songs, which the incomparable Miss Lillie will bring to us this fall. In one of these she is compelled to assume the roguish manners of a slightly depraved child artiste and to lisp a pretty song entitled *A Little Slut Of Six*. Then she will cut loose in a fine romantic ballad, 'The roses have made me remember, What any nice girl would forget', a sweet song that contains the refrain

Just an old-fashioned girl
In an old-fashioned gown
With an old-fashioned stocking
About to come down.

It is interesting to note that Miss Lillie used Noël's *The Roses Have Made Me Remember* in 1930, when talkies were still a rarity, in a Vitaphone short 'programme filler' in which, if his memory served, she opened wide her casement and sang the song with deadpan innocence. She paid no attention to the fact that the casement was slowly but inexorably closing in on her face until it almost hit her, when she very, very gently pushed it wide again. This happened at irregular intervals all through the song. That was all, but the effect was devastating.

The Vortex was as resounding a hit in New York as it had been in London with critics and public again agreeably shocked: 'Nine of the characters are decidedly unpleasant and six of the nine reach depths of moral rottenness seldom presented on the stage before . . . the last scene is highly strung, hysterical, painfully dramatic, leaves the audience in a state of semi-collapse.' *Vogue* thought that this scene would be discussed over many a demi-tasse far into the winter, or even longer.

Once *The Vortex* was thus gratifyingly launched and in spite of a whirlwind of social activity, Noël immediately started work on *Hay Fever*, over which production he said he would rather draw a veil. He, Gladys and his mother, had to sit in a box on the first night and watch Laura Hope Crews overacting to such an extent that she became painfully unfunny, the rest of the cast hardly bothering to act at all, and the audience leaving in twos and threes from the middle of the second act onwards. Not all of them left, however, because the remainder was composed of many friends whom he had invited to attend the party he had over-optimistically decided to give in his own apartment. The atmosphere at the party was

Quite a Lad !

BY MACMICHAEL

Our artist's idea of a day in the life of Mr. Noel Coward, author of "The Vortex," composer, and actor who has arrived: in other words, an "accomplished fact"

How I Write My Songs

By
NOEL COWARD

MUSICAL inspiration is a peculiar sort of thing. It just comes. One cannot sit down and think and think until melodies come to the mind. I am much too busy for that, and, besides, that method would never bring success—at least, not in my case.

I just go on with the business of living, like other people do, until something occurs to me. It may be while I am at dinner, or on a 'bus, or even while I am having a bath. If I am anywhere near a piano I fly to it and play the tune with one hand. That "fixes" it, as a photographer would say, and I can proceed with the rest in a more leisurely way.

The next step is to get the harmony exactly as I want it, playing it over and over again if necessary. After that my task is practically ended. I play it to a trained musician, who writes the notes down and then repeats the piece to me so that I can make quite sure that he has reproduced it correctly.

I may be asked why I do not do this theoretical work myself. How boring! Besides, I happen to know practically nothing about such matters. I have never had a lesson in pianoforte playing in my life. I once went to the Guildhall School of Music for a few lessons in harmony and composition, but found them so dull and tiresome that I gave them up.

One does not need a deep knowledge of the mysteries of theory and musical form in order to compose light songs of the revue and musical comedy type. What *is* necessary is a perfect ear for pleasant sounds. When I think of what seems to me to be a good tune, the most suitable harmony suggests itself at the same time—in a rough form, at any rate. I don't know whether I am breaking conventional rules of theory, and care less. The sound's the thing.

Nearly all my life I have been able to pick tunes up readily after hearing them at a music-hall or theatre, and to play them on the piano. Lots of people can do that to a certain extent, though the difficulty in most cases is to reproduce the

harmony correctly, for every popular success has some little peculiarity in that respect that may cause trouble. But the right gift, an absolutely correct musical ear, solves the problem in a moment.

I do not know when I began to compose, but I must have been very young. I used to write songs in collaboration with Miss Esme Wynne, who has been my friend since my nursery days. She wrote lyrics, and I tried to set them to music. I remember she wrote one which ran :

Our little love is dying,
On his head bloom lately crimson
roses faded quite.

I knew nothing about rhythm in those far-off days; the tune seemed to me the only thing that mattered. The music I

Photo] [*Maurice Beck and Helen Macgregor*
NOEL COWARD

composed caused the words to read like this :

Our little love is dying on his head.
Lately crimson roses faded quite.

Perhaps I was in a hurry. Unfortunately, I have always been pressed for time, and I usually work at a rapid rate. I wrote the whole of "On With the Dance" (now being presented at the London Pavilion)—music, lyrics and book—in a month. My play, "I'll Leave it to You," was written in a few weeks.

It was really through hurry that a certain unfortunate incident happened on the river some time ago. Miss Betty Chester and I were engaged to appear in "The Knight of the Burning Pestle," and as the time for preparation was so short we decided to go to Oxford, where we could study our parts without interruption.

We were in a canoe one day, studying for all we were worth, when the craft upset, and our manuscripts got so wet that they were useless. Result, several days' delay until we obtained new copies.

But I was talking about musical inspiration. One of my greatest successes was "Parisienne Pierrot," sung in "London Calling." The idea of that came to me during a visit to a cabaret in Berlin. I noticed a doll hanging on a curtain, and it seemed to impress itself on my mind. . Soon afterwards, a melody which appeared to associate itself with the doll incident occurred to me, and—well, I just played it.

I thought of the tune of my latest success, "Poor Little Rich Girl," while I was having tea. The usual dash for the piano, and the thing was done. But for some reason I wrote this song in four flats, whereas I had always kept to three flats previously.

There is no scientific explanation of it at all. Some of us have these strange peculiarities, and some have not. I don't even know how I got my musical talent, unless it has been handed down from a grandfather who was organist for many years at the Crystal Palace.

But I wonder if it is fair to his memory to say so ?

Noel Coward's "Clean" Play: "Hay Fever."

Hilda Moore as "Myra Arundel".

Ann Trevor as "Jackie Coryton".

Robin Ervine as "Simon Bliss".

Patrick Susands as "Sandy Tyrell".

Minnie Rayner as "Clara".

Marie Tempest as "Judith Bliss".

W. Graham Browne as "David Bliss".

macabre until alcohol dispelled the chill after an hour or so: Laura Hope Crews remained gracious and charming throughout and gave a much better performance than she had given on the stage. One paper headed its notice HAY FEVER NOTHING TO SNEEZE AT and the comedy 'gently expired' after ailing for a few weeks.

Undaunted, Noël next plunged into *Easy Virtue* with Jane Cowl starring. He purposely set out to write a drawing-room drama (as opposed to 'comedy') with an affectionate backward glance at Pinero and Henry Arthur Jones, but this had several differing results. The critics not unnaturally found the plot 'old-fashioned Pinero', though the play contained quite a lot of Coward comedy: the idea of the beautiful and glamorous Miss Cowl, Paris gowned, settling down to domestic bliss with a hunting set in the shires and upsetting her mother-in-law by leaving Proust's *Sodom And Gomorrah* lying about was funny to begin with: but then Miss Cowl confused the issue by playing with such burning vitality that audiences thrilled to it, and instead of laughs she got tremendous rounds of applause. Right back to Pinero, in fact, which wasn't quite what Noël had intended. Never mind, applause she got in plenty and *Easy Virtue* pleased audiences for months.

Nine days after the New York opening, Noël celebrated his twenty-sixth birthday, after a year crowded with achievements, publicity and popularity, and crowned with the international stardom he had hoped and striven for. One of his newer friends and greatest admirers, Alexander Woollcott, wrote: 'All these triumphs have come to him in his twenty-sixth year. Noël Coward is really younger than anyone with the possible exception of Baby Peggy (a well-known child star of the period), from whom he should be carefully distinguished.'

The pendulum swings, as it must, and 1926 did not start very well with the post-New York tour of *The Vortex*; Newark, Brooklyn and Cincinnatti were kindly enough, but the climax of the play's long-running success was to be six glorious weeks in theatre-loving Chicago, where it would terminate. Noël and Lilian were disconcerted when the comedy of the first act was received in deadly silence, but comforted themselves by deciding that it was a serious audience, in which they could not have been more wrong. When the curtain went up on the tragic third act the sight of Noël in pyjamas set them off, and they split their sides until the curtain came down. 'Never', he wrote, 'since *Charley's Aunt* on a Saturday night in Blackpool, have I heard such hilarious mirth in a theatre.' Trembling with

'There is neither health nor cleanness about any of Mr Coward's characters,' wrote James Agate of Hay Fever *in 1925, 'who are still the same vicious babies sprawling upon the floor of their unwholesome crèche . . . . If rumour is to be believed, Mr Coward wrote this in three days, wearing a flowered dressing-gown and working only before breakfast . . . what I want to know is what kind of work he intends to do after breakfast, when he is clothed and in his right mind?'* Hay Fever *went on to become (with* Blithe Spirit *and* Private Lives) *one of the twenty most commercial and most often-revived British comedies of the century. Bobbie Andrews (right) created the role of Simon Bliss.*

NERMAN

MR. BOBBIE ANDREWS

On tour with The Vortex *and Al Capone-type car, Chicago 1926.*

Opposite above: Noël with friends, America 1925. The toast of Broadway: 'The legend of my modesty grew and grew, until I became quite amazingly unspoiled by my great success.'

Far left: At work in his borrowed New York apartment.

Fred Astaire with two mothers – his own and Noël's – on the Boardwalk in Atlantic City, 1925.

suppressed fury, he wrote NOËL COWARD DIED HERE on the wall of his dressing-room and cut the six weeks' run to an ignoble two. He was sick to death of his demanding part and of the play anyway (though it would, of course, have been better to end in a burst of glory), and it was, in fact at this time that he vowed never again to appear in a play for longer than three months, a vow he kept for the rest of his life.

He had first made the acquaintance of the young, handsome and attractive American, John C. Wilson, during the run of *The Vortex* in London, and this had developed into an intimate friendship during the New York engagement. Jack had become enamoured of the theatre and of Noël to such an extent that he gave up all thoughts of stockbroking, and henceforth devoted himself to Noël's personal management and business interests. Thus it was that to the little England-bound party in the *Olympic* of Noël, Gladys and his mother (plus Noël's first Rolls Royce, which now looks as though he might have bought it from Al Capone in Chicago) was added the witty and charming Jack. Noël admitted to slight fears about whether Lornie would take to or resent Jack's take-over of their hitherto happy-go-lucky handling of his business affairs, but they took to one another on sight: Lornie enjoying Jack's torrent of wisecracks as much as he appreciated her down-to-earth and irreverent jokes. Noël's tight circle of very close friends now consisted of Lornie, Gladys, Joyce Carey and Jack, and, with the exception of Jack (who died in 1961), their friendship proved to be of lifetime endurance.

Joyce, Lilian Braithwaite's daughter, had inherited her mother's beauty and charm but had a wit and keen intelligence of her own, and was also on the stage, having made her first big hit at an early age in the title role of *The*

Young Person In Pink. She was (and is) brilliantly adept at crosswords and pencil and paper parlour-games, and she and Noël went so far as to invent a code which was never broken, even by the greatest code decipherers in the land. This continued for many years until Princess Marina, speaking for everybody else, said, '*You* may be having great fun, but you're boring us all to death.' They also had a language of their own in which other people could participate and which was in consequence much more fun. Noël gave Joyce a gold cigarette case inscribed:

BOB THIS MARGARET BLANCHE ADHESS
THROUGH THE EDITH BOURCHIER JESSIE
JANE'S YOUR JUSTICE WILLIAM S.
FOR IT TUBB'S MY RONALD BESSIE *

And so Joyce slipped easily into the others' habit of putting even their most fleeting thoughts into verse in which it was understood that sickening flattery should be mingled with abuse. Noël was by this time being jokingly called 'the Master' by the circle, which also gave them another name easier to rhyme than the difficult Noël. In the face of the vilification she received from the Master, Lornie (who possessed none of these attributes) insisted that she was beautiful, slim and lithe, with dancing eyes and luxuriant tresses:

Lornie is a silly-billy
O my *God* is Lornie silly
Lorn is sillier than Willy
Graham-Browne and he *is* silly.

Master on the other hand is witty
Talented and *very* pretty
Prettier than Dame May Whitty
And God knows she's *really* pretty.

Lornie was forced to sing her own praises in this answer, written as though from the Master:

Through all these weary working days
Of toil and strife and strain
There's one who all fatigue allays
And makes me gay again.

Her dainty happy little face
Is Youth personified
I really could not stand the pace
Without her by my side.

Her lissom grace enchants my eyes
When I am tired and worn
I *cannot* over-emphasize
My gratitude to Lorn.

From Noël, who had been given a toy seal with a coat of beige bristles:

This tiny baby seal new born
Reminds me in a way of Lorn
There's something in its dusty hair
Its glassy and forbidding stare
That makes a picture clear and plain
Of fascinating Lorn Loraine.

*By way of explanation: Bob Hope, film star; Margaret Case, N.Y. editor of Vogue; Blanche Sweet, silent film star; Myra Hess, pianist; Edith Sharp, actress; Chilli Bourchier, film star; Jessie Winter, actress; Jane Comfort, actress; Justice Darling, judge famous for his severity; William S. Hart, silent film cowboy star; Carrie Tubb, contralto; Ronald True, murderer; Bessie Love, film and stage star. All famous or very well known in their time. Answer: Hope this case sweet admirer | Through the sharp chilly winter | Comforts your darling heart | For it carries my true love.

'A Defence' by Lorn:

Though you think I'm old and jaded
For my charms are not paraded
I would have you realize
Many think I am a prize.
E. Maria Albanesi
Thinks I am perfect daisy
And I *can* dance Irish jigs on
The emotions of Nell Higson.
Yes, although I fail to please
Sutherlands and Angleseys
And the Pembrokes find me stale,
I am friends with Betty Shale.

The Master – 'Thoughts On Waking':

Here I sweetly lie in bed
And wait for Lornie's dancing tread.
Here in bed I sweetly lie
Anticipating Lornie's high
Well-modulated, senseless bray
Mouthing the topics of the day.

Lornie sent him a note to herald her approach:

The answer to your deepest prayers
Is now advancing up the stairs.
A lovely lady dressed in blue
Will come to have a chat with you.

As far as his private life was concerned, Noël was happy to be home again, and with every reason: Jack made an instant social success and they were greatly in demand for Debrett-studded parties and weekends in stately homes. The circle of friends was so close-knit that they would from now on be known as 'the family', and Noël's financial position could be described for the first time as better than solvent. He revelled in having a Rolls-Royce of his own to drive – when it wasn't being repaired at the factory in Derby, which happened too often for his liking. He began to find the little cottage at Dockenfield too pokey, and his thoughts turned to Romney Marsh in Kent, where he and his mother had been so happy four years before with a 'ten shillings a week roof over our heads' and near the sea, which was much to be desired. It was a neighbour, a Mr Body, from this same locality who wrote out of the blue after some months of fruitless searching to say he wanted to let his farmhouse at Aldington for £50 a year. They took it 'until they found something better', as they thought at the time, but it turned out to be ideally situated on rising land which gave a panoramic view right across the marsh to the sea. And so, a few years later, Noël bought Goldenhurst outright together with the many acres of grazing pasture and woodland surrounding it, enlarged and beautified it, and it remained his dearly loved country home for thirty years.

What was left of 1926 passed busily and pleasantly enough, except for two further skirmishes with censorship which, idiotic though they were, added enormously to what is now called 'the buzz' about Noël's plays. Jane Cowl arrived in England swathed in leopard-skins, orchids and glamour to find that the Manchester Watch Committee resolutely refused to allow Noël to use such a suggestive title at their Opera House as *Easy Virtue*, though the next-door cinema was unconcernedly showing a film called *Flames Of Passion*. All of which fanned the excitement. Noël was allowed to use the title *Easy Virtue* by the time it opened in London; Miss Cowl let off her full display of histrionic fireworks as effectively as she had in New York; James Agate described her beautiful face as a battleground for the emotions; and she played to applauding audiences until she felt homesick and returned to New York.

The same happened with *The Queen Was In The Parlour*, two and a half months later. Noël loved the books of Anthony Hope, especially *The Prisoner of Zenda*, and because of his admiration, allowed himself this charming excursion into Ruritania. Whatever may be said of the play, Noël proved that he had without question become a past-master in the art of providing larger-than-life personality stars with vehicles which would enhance them and their gifts still further. This is yet another of his talents which has seldom been equalled and, whatever the evils of the star-system may be, there is no doubt that this particular talent at the same time enabled him to ensure that the other actors in the cast, however small their roles, were given 'effective' parts to play with one or two advantageous chances.

Noël had written the star part of Queen Nadya especially for Madge Titheradge; he had idolized her ever since he played with her in *Peter Pan* and seen her in a Drury Lane melodrama in which she had cried 'Away! Away, along the Great North Road, for Liberty! for Life! for Love!' and then jumped on a motorbike to go and save the situation. One then actually saw her long, daring drive in front of a revolving cyclorama, after which – although the bike had been ridden by a double – Miss Titheradge came forward to great applause, panting for breath and mopping her brow with exhaustion. She therefore played the Queen, not with Miss Cowl's flamboyance, but with her own brand of suppressed power and emotion. Noël said she illuminated the whole play with her magic and was grateful to her for its success.

Basil Dean persuaded Noël, against his will, to appear in *The Constant Nymph* in September. The play was the big hit of the year but Noël hated every moment of it from the first rehearsal onwards; he thought the experience must have been good for him because the part of Lewis Dodd was unlike anything he had ever before attempted. Supposedly a young composer of genius, Noël thought Dodd an insensitive oaf, puffing away at a pipe and, worst of all for Noël, wearing purposely ill-fitting clothes. He

The Constant Nymph, 1926: Noël played three weeks as Lewis Dodd (with Edna Best as the 'nymph') and was then replaced by John Gielgud in his first starring West End role.

ALL OVER BETWEEN FLORENCE AND LEWIS: (L. TO R.) TERESA SANGER (MISS EDNA BEST), FLORENCE CHURCHILL (MISS CATHLEEN NESBITT), AND LEWIS DODD (MR. NOEL COWARD)

received much praise for his performance, played for three weeks, and then collapsed from nervous exhaustion. His part was taken over by his young understudy John Gielgud, who played with conviction and success for the rest of the very long run.

Noël's breakdown was attributed to the strain imposed upon his nerves by the almost continuous stresses of the past two years. He was put to bed by his doctors and for a week was allowed to see nobody, and then, against everyone's advice, he insisted on sailing for New York because rehearsals for *This Was A Man* could be postponed no longer. While he was on the high seas, the first play he wrote, at the age of eighteen, *The Rat Trap*, was produced at Hampstead – a major mistake, which was taken off after only twelve performances.

This Was A Man, with Francine Larrimore starring, fared little better in New York. When questioned about the play in later years, Noël had retained only two memories of it: one was that Basil Dean had directed it at such a snail's pace that one had time to go to the corner and get an ice-cream soda between every line, and the other was Lornie's opinion, when asked, of Miss Larrimore – 'She has scrutinized herself minutely from every angle and has been unable to detect a flaw.'

The play has a curious history. In England the Lord Chamberlain banned it completely, principally because when told of his wife's adultery in the last act, the husband bursts out laughing. ('The English like the Commandments to be broken seriously', was Noël's comment.) The play was treated with a certain amount of importance in other quarters, however: the great Max Reinhardt presented Rudolf Kommer's adaptation of it in Berlin as *Die Ehe Von Welt*. It was also done in Paris by Edward Stirling's English Players, where it broke all (their) records: extra police had to be called out to control the crowds, swollen by English visitors fighting to get in to see a new Coward play so *risqué* that it had been banned in London. The handsome Mr Stirling kept *This Was A Man* in his repertory for five years, but the play has never, so far as is known, been produced in England.

Noël, still in America, had by no means recovered from his breakdown. Always having enjoyed the best of health and spirits, he was at a loss to understand the lassitude verging on melancholia, the headaches and the nerves continuously on edge. He went to White Sulphur Springs for peace and rest, and while there wrote *The Marquise* for Marie Tempest, but, although the play had got itself on to paper quite easily, he returned to New York uncured. He felt strongly that he must for the time being get away from the theatre and from everybody and everything he knew; so he bought himself a ticket for Hong Kong, going via San Francisco and Hawaii. He got as far as Hawaii, where he collapsed completely, and a wise doctor ordered him to rest for a month at a lonely ranch belonging to friends, set in the midst of their banana and sugar plantations. He began to sleep soundly for the first time in many weeks and, during the soothing month in that benign air, he not only began to improve in health but also had time to lecture himself severely on past mistakes and to chart his future. Never again would he waste his energy and dissipate his vitality unnecessarily: people made too many demands on them in his private life, especially socially – they were assets too precious and must be conserved for his work in the theatre, and for his writing. Work was the answer. Only in work was true contentment to be found; any other happiness was a bonus well-earned.

By the time he began to long to exchange the tropics for the gentler greens of England he knew he had cured himself, and in the process had learnt other notable lessons. He had learned to be self-reliant and self-sufficient, that in fact he had a positive need to be alone occasionally and

The disaster that was Sirocco: *'On the first night', writes Raymond Massey, 'I saw three different fist-fights between Noël's admirers and those who thought he was already finished as a playwright. At the curtain call Frances Doble made the immortal comment, "This is the happiest night of my life."' Below: Ivor Novello in* Sirocco.

The enfant gâté of the studio: Ivor Novello as a lap dog.

enjoy it – 'to recharge the batteries'. To satisfy this need, he became henceforth an incurable travel addict: he would always have a plan to get to faraway places immediately after a new production had been launched, or after one of his spells of acting, or if he became too emotionally involved. 'Good old geographical distance, that'll do the trick!' he would say. And, for him, it always did.

As a consequence of these decisions to take greater care of himself physically, he did not appear on the stage at all during 1927. It was for other reasons that 1927 came to be known and remembered as DISASTER Year. He spent some pleasant summer weeks at Goldenhurst writing a light comedy called *Home Chat*, and with its production in October came the first calamity. Noël, Madge Titheradge and Basil Dean thought it was good, an opinion shared by nobody except themselves. It was, in fact, received with sustained booing from the gallery and died an early death, unmourned. Far worse was to come four weeks later with *Sirocco*, a play he had written six years before, inspired, – if that is the word – by a rather tawdry *festa* he had attended at Rapallo. The *festa* one saw on the stage was described as about as cheerful as a conference of undertakers, the dialogue as dreary, and the only time the audience enjoyed themselves was during Ivor Novello's passionate love scene with Frances Doble, when they shrieked with mirth and made sucking noises as the couple were kissing, interspersed with catcalls and raspberries. Chaos prevailed in the theatre all through the last act and the curtain fell to a furore of hisses and boos, made worse, much louder and more prolonged by Noël's mistaken bravery in going on stage to take his 'author's call' and staying there until the hullaballoo subsided. But the abuse continued in the street from the hostile crowd, who had waited for Noël to come out of the stage door. *Sirocco* was the most catastrophic débâcle of Noël's career, ranking with

Sam Behrman's four-handed comedy The Second Man: *with Noël and Raymond Massey were Zena Dare and Ursula Jeans. 'All plays should have a cast of four,' wrote* The Times, *'no more, no less.'*

A Play of Four Characters:
"The Second Man," at the Playhouse.

"I'VE COME TO KILL YOU, CLARK STOREY": MR. RAYMOND MASSEY AS AUSTIN LOWE, AND MR. NOEL COWARD AS CLARK STOREY.

MONICA GREY TELLS CLARK STOREY THAT HE IS THE FATHER OF HER UNBORN CHILD: MR. NOEL COWARD AS STOREY, AND MISS URSULA JEANS AS MONICA GREY.

"This Year of Grace," at the London Pavilion.

"TEACH ME TO DANCE LIKE GRANDMA USED TO DANCE. SIXTY SUMMERS AGO"

Mr. Jack Holland, Miss Jean Barry, Mr. Sonnie Hale, Miss Tilly Losch, Miss Maisie Gay, Mr. Douglas Byng, Miss Joan Ca.
Mr. Lance Lister, and Others

the first night of *The Vortex* but for the opposite reason: both nights were set apart in his memory for ever.

Although *Sirocco* was the only occasion when Ivor Novello and Noël worked together professionally, they enjoyed a rumbustious friendship from the first time they met, in Manchester in 1917. Laughter and Ivor inevitably went together; something funny always happened. Noël came back from every visit to Ivor at Redroofs with more remarks to find a permanent place in his memory and in his vocabulary: 'Oh, what gorgeous gravy!' Ivor had cried in the middle of luncheon, and then at tea in front of the same rather grand and stuffy guests it was, 'Now the sugar's buggered off!' Ivor appeared rather surprisingly in *Henry V* at Drury Lane and Adrianne Allen took her little son, Daniel Massey, for his Shakespeare initiation. He looked at the programme picture of Ivor's beautiful face beneath Harry's crown and said, 'Mummy, why is that lady wearing that funny hat?', which of course Ivor enjoyed as much as anybody.

After the beatings Noël had taken from the disastrous failures of *Home Chat* and *Sirocco*, he was not unnaturally beset by certain fears. Perhaps he really had stretched himself too thin, attempted too much too soon? Perhaps he was, after all, as the Press were only too ready to suggest, a flash in the pan who had already written himself out at the age of twenty-seven? He had committed himself to appear in Sam Behrman's comedy *The Second Man* in two months' time, another ordeal slowly approaching which would have to be faced. Would he again be booed off the stage, especially as he had to portray an author destroying his manuscript with a cry of 'Trash!'? On the contrary, when the dreaded moment came and he made his first entrance, he was greeted with applause and the reviews pronounced the play a success and praised him for his acting – a wry pleasure, for some critics made it clear that they would willingly exchange so 'uncertain' a writer for so good an actor.

Jessie Matthews in
"This Year of Grace."

THE NOEL COWARD TUNE THE PRINCE LIKED.

A Room with a View, and you, and no one to wor-ry us no one to hur-ry us through this dream we've found. We'll gaze at the sky, and try to guess what it's all a-bout, then we will fig-ure out why the world is round. ___

Published by Chappell & Co.

"A Room with a View," the tune from "This Year of Grace," written and composed by Noel Coward, which was played nine times at the Ascot Cabaret Ball at the wish of the Prince of Wales, who was dancing there.

This Year of Grace: *first of the Cochran–Coward revues at the London Pavilion, 1928. The score included* A Room With A View, Dance Little Lady, World Weary *and* Mary Make-Believe. *The cast included Maisie Gay, Sonnie Hale and his soon-to-be-wife Jessie Matthews, Tilly Losch, Douglas Byng and a young Sheilah Graham.*

Right and overleaf: Bitter Sweet, *the operette of Noël's career and possibly of the British stage this century. 'Tiara'd women clapped till the seams of their gloves burst,' wrote* The Tatler *of the first night in 1929; 'the older generation could say with more complacency than truth that this was how they had fallen in love, and the younger generation were made to wonder if in rejecting romance they might not have missed something.'*

Charles Cochran remained staunchly supportive of Noël all through the months of failure, and insisted that he should continue with their plans for the next Cochran revue, going so far as to entrust him for the first time with the entire show – sketches, music and lyrics. Noël rose to the challenge and Lornie lit upon a perfect title: *This Year Of Grace.* The two big hit songs, evergreen to this day, were *A Room With A View*, written at, of all unlikely places, the lonely ranch in Hawaii, and *Dance Little Lady* with biting lyrics set to an insistently danceable tune, and with the chorus costumed by Oliver Messel, their faces masked to represent their empty, fashionable boredom. The revue was a stream of beauty and delight, heightened by sensational dancing ranging from the balletic to the acrobatic, its elegance offset by the lowest of low comedy from Douglas Byng and the rich, rowdy Maisie Gay. Such a success was it that Noël jumped at the chance to go to New York that autumn and appear in it with that nonpareil, Beatrice Lillie. He introduced his wistful *World Weary* into it specially for her, which she sang as a little office boy perched on a high stool with, he said, infinite pathos while munching an apple.

This Year Of Grace was the first of a series of triumphs Noël shared with

CHANSON DE LA CREVETTE

IF LOVE WERE ALL

JANE MARNAC

PRÉSENTE

AU TEMPS DES VALSES

BITTER○SWEET

à l'APOLLO · PARIS·

JE VOUS REVERRAI
   (I'LL SEE YOU AGAIN) DUO

CHANSON DE LA CREVETTE
   (IF LOVE WERE ALL)

ABANDONNÉE
   (KISS ME)

TZIGANE
   (ZIGEUNER)

NOTRE PETIT CAFÉ
   (DEAR LITTLE CAFÉ) DUO

TOKAY

Créé par

YO MAUREL

LIVRET ET LYRIQUES DE
SAINT○GRANIER
MUSIQUE DE
NOËL COWARD

CHAPPELL
(E. A.)
ÉDITEURS DE MUSIQUE
22, Boulevard Haussemann, 22
PARIS-VIII°

Prix:
10 fr.

PUBLICATIONS FRANCIS○DAY, 30, RUE DE L'ÉCHIQUIER PARIS

CHAPPELL & C° LTD, LONDON, W.I.

The TATLER

Vol. CXVIII. No. 1532. London, November 5, 1930. POSTAGE: Inland, 2½d.; Canada and Newfoundland, 1½d.; Foreign, 8½d. Price One Shilling

Noel COWARD

CHARLES B. COCHRAN

has the honour to announce

THE FIRST ANNIVERSARY

of

Noel COWARD'S

Exquisite Operette

BITTER SWEET

at

HIS MAJESTY'S THEATRE JULY 18TH

at 8:30 o'clock

BITTER . . . to lose PEGGY
SWEET . . . to regain EVELYN

Miss Evelyn Laye being greeted on her arrival at Waterloo by Miss Peggy Wood and Mr. C. B. Cochran. The return of Miss Laye from the States to take up the part created by Miss Peggy Wood in Noel Coward's triumphant success has its sad as well as its glad side. While welcoming with rapture the second "Lady Shayne" straight from the plaudits of New York, London will gratefully remember the brilliant rendering of her predecessor, who, after playing this exacting rôle for fifteen months, has been ordered a rest. Au revoir and many, many thanks to Peggy. Pass friend Evelyn; all's well. Another picture of Miss Laye appears on a later page

Peggy Wood for London, Evelyn Laye for New York, Jane Marnac for Paris: all played Sari (as did Jeanette MacDonald and Anna Neagle on film) in a score which featured If Love Were All, I'll See You Again, Zigeuner, Ladies of The Town *and* Dear Little Café. *In London alone Bitter Sweet ran for 697 performances.*

Cochran during the following six years. The second was *Bitter-Sweet* in 1929 with which Noël rounded off 'his' decade, an out and out victory over the prophets who, two years before, had foretold his doom. Noël had chosen, with uncanny accuracy, the exact moment when the public – unaware of it themselves – would welcome a change from the jazzy musicals of the Twenties. *Bitter-Sweet* was on a much larger scale and quite unlike anything he had ventured on before: a full-blown operette, drenched with melody and sparkling with witty point numbers and the excitement of Viennese waltzes. It was his farewell to the Twenties and it remains his best and his best-loved musical.

AS SARAH MILLICK : MISS PEGGY WOOD IN 1875 FASHIONS.

AS SARI LINDEN : MISS PEGGY WOOD IN 1880 FASHIONS.

AS THE MARCHIONESS OF SHAYNE : MISS PEGGY WOOD IN 1930 FASHIONS.

3
THE
THIRTIES

THE YEAR 1930 FOUND NOËL INSTALLED IN 17 GERALD ROAD, Belgravia; he had at last left his riotously-coloured suite of rooms at 111 Ebury Street and had bought the lease of what was to become familiarly known as The Studio – the only residence he ever owned in London. This was actually two houses, for he also bought the lease of 1 Burton Mews, which backed on to it, conveniently containing an office for Lornie, a kitchen, rooms for the staff and a garage beneath. The long cement approach from Gerald Road to the front door of No. 17 – grandly referred to as the courtyard – ensured privacy and quiet: quiet enough for Noël to be able to compose when he wanted to, which was important. Indoors, on one side of the spacious studio itself there was an almost stage-size dais boasting two grand pianos, and above it a window of vast proportions which cost a fortune to curtain and another fortune in window-cleaners. The overall result of this made it a theatrically effective setting for the many large parties Noël was to give there until he left to live abroad twenty-six years later. Virtually every great singer of the period sang from that dais, and every great musician played the pianos: Toscanini, Rachmaninov (he and Noël formed a mutual admiration society), Cole Porter, Richard Rodgers – and even Fritz Kreisler played jazz. With The Studio set so far back from the road, Noël and his party guests could make almost as much noise as they liked, but not quite: in the early hours the friendly local police station would sometimes ring to say that Mr Coward and his guests had delighted them and the neighbours long enough. The officers were always gentle with this suggestion, having been part of the party: looking after the guests car-parking in the small street and then listening to Ethel Merman, Judy Garland, Lena Horne or Tauber or Yvonne Printemps through the open windows. When he left The Studio for good in 1956, Noël recalled 'the mornings after opening nights, the interminable telephone conversations, the ideas conceived and the plans made, and above all the jokes, the rich wonderful jokes with Lorn and Cole and Graham roaring with laughter ... I hope that whoever occupies that lovely place will have as happy and gay a time in it as I have had.'

Gertrude Lawrence and Noël Coward opened the smart, brand-new Phoenix Theatre with *Private Lives* in September 1930. The words 'famous', 'success' and '*Private Lives*' seem to have gone together from the start. The fact that Noël had written it in four days, while recovering from a bad attack of influenza in the Cathay Hotel in Shanghai, soon became famous, as did Gertie's cable after he enthusiastically sent her the script, NOTHING WRONG THAT CAN'T BE FIXED, and so did his terse reply, NOTHING TO BE FIXED EXCEPT YOUR PERFORMANCE. They were both well aware that they were on to a good thing and Gertie presumably gladly put up with a lot of leg-pulling from the time of her high-handed cable until rehearsals started:

Dear Miss Lawrence,
   With regard to your illiterate scrawl of the 14th inst., Mr Coward asks me to say that there was talk of you playing a small part in a play of his on condition that you

The studio in Gerald Road, Noël's London home until the early 1950s.

tour and find your own clothes (same to be of reasonable quality) and that you understudy Jessie Matthews whom you have always imitated. Mr Coward will be visiting some rather important people in the South of France in mid-July and he will appear at Cap d'Ail, whether you like it or not, on the 20th. ... Several complicated contracts are being sent to you on the terms you agreed upon – i.e. £6.10.0 a week and understudy.

Many of the lines from *Private Lives* have become famous in their own right; 'Moonlight can be cruelly deceptive', 'Very flat, Norfolk', 'Women should be struck regularly, like gongs' and so on, but the line most loved and quoted is 'Strange how potent cheap music is', and one wonders why? Perhaps it is because, as Edward Albee points out, Noël always wrote with truth and this, although a small truth, is a pertinent and universal one. Lord Byron, writing in Ravenna in 1821, was moved by this same potency: 'Oh! there is an organ playing in the street – a waltz too! I must leave off to listen. They are playing a waltz which I have heard ten thousand times at the balls in London. ... Music is a strange thing.' Strange that Lord Byron should also have used the word and that he and Noël should both have been moved by a waltz: the waltz from *Private Lives* is *Someday I'll Find You*, one of Noël's most evocative and tender love songs. In passing, in most published editions of the play the line is given as 'Extraordinary how potent ...', but this is incorrect: Noël and Gertie made the definitive recording of *Private Lives* on 1 May 1930 – the word they used is 'strange'.

Gerald Road – Noël dining with Lornie – and a chair that was later to travel with him around the world before they both ended up in Switzerland: occupants along the way included Sir John Gielgud.

When Gertie died in 1952, Noël wrote for *The Times*:

I wish . . . that I could have seen her just once more playing in a play of mine, for no one I have ever known, however brilliant and however gifted, has contributed quite what she contributed to my work. Her quality was to me unique and her magic imperishable. An analysis of her talent, however, would require a more detached pen than mine. I could never be really detached about Gertie if I tried to the end of my days. We have grown up in the theatre together, and now she is suddenly dead and I am left with a thousand memories of her, not one of which will ever fade. I have loved her always, as herself and as an artist.

After *Private Lives*, Noël's next triumph, spectacular in every sense of the word, was *Cavalcade* at Drury Lane in October 1931. No one who saw the production will ever forget it. For pageantry, poignancy, magnificence of scale, range of scenes and of characters it will remain Noël's greatest achievement in the theatre. His use of the stage for the twenty-two scene changes (he directed the enormous production himself, greatly helped by Gladys, whose designs for the sets and costumes were in themselves perfection) was a technical marvel. There was, at that time, a great fear that the novelty of 'the talkies' would prove a serious threat to live theatre and among all the praise Noël received there were more than a few gleeful comments like 'Your production beats the cinema into a cocked hat!'. The papers would go on lauding Noël for his brilliant use of the revolving stage, which made Mr Cochran angry (he had counted forty-five of these mis-statements), though actually it was unwittingly a great compliment: all Noël had used was the six existing hydraulic stage-lifts, which had been in use for nearly thirty years; there was then no revolving stage at Drury Lane.

There was, however, argument about the merits of *Cavalcade* as a play, some of the fault-finding coming from condescending left-wing critics, who saw in it nothing but jingoism which, they said, Noël had calculated to coincide with a General Election that happened to result in a victory for the National Government. The only thing that escaped notice in the uproar, Noël pointed out with truth, was that *Cavalcade*, apart from its appeal as a spectacle, possessed several finely written scenes which had both dignity and brevity. The tumult and the paeans of praise built up to a crescendo during the next two weeks until Noël felt uncomfortably that he was being made into a national hero – 'Coward's Call To The Youth Of The Nation' and so on – that the glory had become tin-pot, and that the time had come for him to disappear.

His wanderlust never lay dormant for long. He had already 'done' the Far East with his 'ideal travelling companion', Jeffery Amherst, and this time they decided on South America, sailing from Boulogne in a German-Spanish ship bound for Rio de Janeiro, to drift over that vast continent for nine months with no settled itinerary. 'We've done nothing but eat and sleep since we got on board. The food is beyond belief delicious. The feeling of freedom and peace is divine – absolutely nothing to do. I can hardly believe it.'

After three socially hectic weeks in Rio, they went on to São Paulo and then Buenos Aires, from whence they made expeditions and began to see the things they had travelled so far for – jungles, llamas, turgid tropical rivers, squawking coloured parakeets, vast mountains, Inca ruins, deserts and languorous Latin-American cities. They watched the source of the Amazon babbling out from under a few pebbles, got to the Iguassu Falls, but couldn't see them properly for the mists of white spray and black mosquitoes, and to Lake Titicaca where the local native ladies delighted Noël by wearing bowler hats, 'every man jack of them'.

He has left many vignettes: Jeffery and he made a long, uncomfortable journey to a remote railhead on their way to Valparaiso, and had to wait more long hours for the train, watching their fellow travellers. 'There were some noisy types who sounded as though they were planning a revolution, an enormously fat priest mopping his face, a young couple dressed to the nines, two hirsute tiny sailors and a florid lady with a basket in which there were three hens and a baby. Every now and then the baby shrieked, whereupon she disentangled it from the hens and jammed its face against a yellowish gas-globe which she produced from inside her bodice.'

Noël had begun his lifelong association with the Royal Navy two years before, when, having completed *Private Lives*, he and Jeffery were invited by the Captain to travel as guests in the warship HMS *Suffolk* for the five-

EVERY PICTURE TELLS A STORY
Amanda (Miss Gertrude Lawrence) and Elyot
(Mr. Noel Coward) meet and love is re-born

THE PLAY

With which are incorporated
"THE PLAY," "THE PLAY SOUVENIR," "THE STAGE SOUVENIR"

ICTORIAL

"CAVALCADE"

VOL. LIX

o. 57

MONTHLY

NOEL COWARD

The King sees 'Cavalcade'

DRURY LANE SCENES

Great Outburst of Loyalty

'NATIONAL ANTHEM' FERVOUR

By Our Special Representative

Their Majesties the King and Queen attended a performance of "Cavalcade" at Drury Lane last night.

That is to state in the simplest terms that there was last night an outburst of loyalty, a welling up of love for England and faith in English destiny such as has rarely moved and quickened the heart of London since the War.

The toast from Cavalcade, *Noël's one and only Drury Lane epic: 'Let's couple the future of England with the past of England . . . and let's drink to the hope that one day this country of ours, which we love so much, will find dignity and greatness and peace again.'*

A PLAY WHICH MAKES ME RAGE

Ethel Mannin

expresses her own views for which the Editor does not take responsibility.

Some of us don't thrill to that sort of thing, that sort of hysterical, sentimental, mob-feeling which passes as "patriotism."

After Mafeking we come to the next large war, and then we are shown another "big scene," in which columns of khaki-clad men march in endless circles at the back of the stage, whilst three young women at the front of the stage screech out the popular songs of the time. The marching men sing "Tipperary" . . . nothing, you see has been omitted that might be calculated to bring a sob to every throat and to stir the pulse with patriotic fervour.

Only, as I say, some of us don't react quite that way to that sort of thing. Rage burns in some of us, rage at this capitalising of the tragedy and horror of war, disgust at the sentimentalising of something unspeakably dreadful.

Fond Mamma and Queen Victoria

After this we are shown Victoria Station and the arrival of a troop train, and the departure of one with men going out to France. Fond Mamma, whose little boy who played with soldiers has now grown-up and is ripe for gun-fodder, . . . his way with a brave . . . strolling

If I had ever had any doubts about joining up with a fight[ing] [So]cialist Party, Mr. Noel Coward['s] . . . have settled it for . . . days of war-time . . . [per]secution of consci[ence] . . . I felt so sick. "Ca[valcade] . . . revival of that same . . . a Union Jack round . . . perpetuates the spir[it] . . . is to me the most . . . most tragic part . . . great British public . . . mother's milk! But . . . what an audience . . . industrial areas wo[uld] . . . their womenfolk, . . . youth that has nev[er] . . . privilege of the rig[ht] . . .

The Story of C[avalcade]

For the benefit [of those who have] not seen this jing[o] . . . you something a[bout] . . . scenes shows a l[ittle boy] with toy soldier[s] . . . British Mamma . . . Later we see . . . and the news . . . is announced; . . . scene" of th[e] . . . the National . . . stage audien[ce] . . . the actual au[dience] . . . rises to its fe[et] . . . liant spectac[le] . . . feet" singing . . . they are wor[th] . . . "Auld Lang [Syne]" . . .

in "Cavalcade" is when the faithful old retainer of a housekeeper shows a change of attitude after the war and no longer calls fat Mamma "your ladyship" or "Ma'am." It is shown in such a way that it is obvious that we are meant to deplore the passing of servility in servants . . . all round me were fat, white, bejewelled and befurred women whom one felt sure were thanking Mr. Coward for showing up the facts that servants are no longer what they were, and feeling how nice and sympathetic of him it was to put this little touch in.

If only one could have felt that Coward was making this point as a challenge to class distinctions, if only he had given the faithful old retainer dignity and used the opportunity to put *the upper classes* in their place for once. . . . But Noel Coward is now a very successful young man, and sometimes success makes people forget, so that they instinctively ally themselves on the side of money and power. It is a case of other times, other company—and another point of view. Were there no servant girls in the gallery to cry out in anger when fat Mamma was rebuking her no longer servile old retainer—none to cry out, "And a dam' good thing, too!" in favour of this new spirit of independence?

[The] Gallery Loves It!

[. . . I repeat] . . . are even . . . s, blood- . . . [m]eans a . . . it is the . . . spread . . . [gos]pel of the . . . work our . . . hand and . . . [that] time. New . . . [socia]list-organ- . . . [ab]out Soviet . . . [thi]s country . . . with doles, . . . [go]vernments, . . . [wh]ich "Caval-

---

THEATRE ROYAL

DRURY LANE

MANAGING DIRECTOR · GEORGE GROSSMITH

NIGHTLY for time see Daily Papers.
MATS.: MON. WED. & SAT. AT 2-30.

IN ASSOCIATION WITH
THEATRE ROYAL
DRURY LANE

CHARLES B. COCHRAN

PRESENTS

Cavalcade

BY NOEL COWARD

PRODUCED BY THE AUTHOR

BETWEEN MAESTROS: Autori's pictorial interview with Noel Coward

SIGNOR FERNANDO AUTORI, the well-known operatic bass who is also a caricaturist, recently called on Mr. Noel Coward between the acts of "Private Lives" at the Phoenix Theatre. He supplements the above pictorial impressions with the following verbal account :—

Punctually at the minute, Mr. Noel Coward shakes my hand in his dressing room. He wears a rich make-up costume of vest and pant. "Maestro Autori," he say. "Maestro Coward," say I. Then, with great and friendly politeness, he tells me many pretty things, speaking in Italian, French and English all at the same time. He is not at all embarrassed by his slight costume, knowing I wish to sketch him all around the compass. His face in talking changes a thousand expressions, and I regret my pencil is not a movie pencil to depict all of them.

The telephone rings and rings, and Signor Coward has for each occasion the lovely phrase with darling in it. Then it is time for him to go to the stage ; I follow him to the wings until the last minute, while someone put on his coat and someone else stick a cigarette in a cigarette holder in his mouth. On the stage, he is as lively as in the dressing room—plays piano, quarrels with his Signorina Gertrude Lawrence, has his head knocked with a Master's Voice, and many other troubles.

Back in dressing room he offers me cigarettes, whisky sodas, everything—presents me to all the artists, talking, talking all the time. His desire is to meet Mussolini, know what I think of the show, is there sentiment sufficient in the singing, would an Italian audience find him sympatico . . . To all I say "Yes," because I think so, and because he leave me no time for to say more.

So we smoke and drink to our comradeliness. Finally, he produces photograph for me and flourishes on it "To Fernando from Noel"; and Mister Coward and Signor Autori melt away in friendly "Arriverderci Fernando," "Arriverderla Noel"

Visiting Hollywood in 1932: Fairbanks and Coward – a friendship of thirty years; with Joan Crawford (below); Mae West and Cary Grant.

Photographed on board. R.M.S. "QUEEN MARY."

Shipboard meetings (left to right): Laurence Olivier, Anna Neagle (twice) and Leslie Howard, Meriel Forbes and Ralph Richardson, and Lady Ravensdale at the bar.

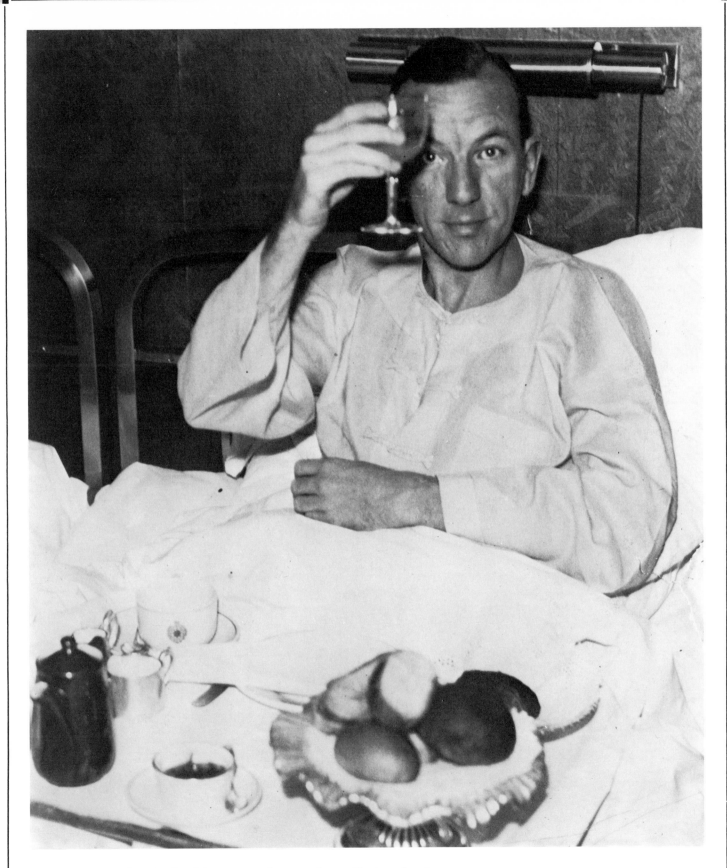

Christmas 1930: hospitalized in Sweden, having closed his finger in a door at Prince William's festive gathering. Another guest (see signature) was Garbo who, for reasons best known to herself, referred to Noël thereafter as 'My little bridegroom'.

Greta Garbo

"And then we'll do that bit from Private Lives."

day voyage from Shanghai to Hong Kong. Their few days in Valparaiso were again enlivened by the Navy: a light cruiser and two destroyers happened to be in, and they were soon involved in a merry-go-round of naval occasions, formal and informal parties on board, a whole day of gunnery practice fifty miles out to sea, 'a couple of fairly libidinous guest nights' and other marine junketings.

Noël was startled one lazy afternoon in the garden of the British Embassy in Santiago by an abrupt cable from the Lunts: OUR CONTRACT WITH THEATRE GUILD UP IN JUNE WHAT ABOUT IT? Eleven years had gone by since he and the Lunts had made their pact. Now it was up to him to carry out the most difficult part of it – to write a sparkling vehicle for the three of them. He had, however, five months in which, surely, an idea would drop into his head and so he shut his mind to the problem and decided to enjoy what remained of his holiday:

We encountered strange birds and beasts including a herd of carpinchos, which are of the guinea-pig family and the size of Shetland ponies; they are also riddled with lice and are extremely friendly. I recall a moment of particular enchantment when we stopped in bright moonlight to stretch our legs. An enormous valley spread all around us encircled by snow-capped mountains under a sky blazing with stars. The silence was awe-inspiring, broken only by an occasional cough from a herd of llamas grazing nearby. We felt we were on top of the world and it was with reluctance that we climbed back into our bizarre vehicle, [a Ford car adapted to run on a railway track] and continued our journey to Arequipa and drew up before the Quinta Bates.

The Quinta Bates was – unlikely that it still exists – a guest house famous in its time for its haphazard comfort and even more famous for its proprietress, a redoubtable lady known to one and all as 'Tia' Bates. She was waiting up for Jeff and Noël in a red merino dressing-gown, with tea and hot-water bottles at the ready, grey hair run wild, twinkling eyes and an air of distinction: cosy landlady and Grand Duchess in one. Noël adored her on sight. Dead long since, she and her guest house had *aficionados* the world over, judging from the people Noël ran into many years after. Mention of the Quinta Bates made strangers at once become reunited members of some curious club, and over many years Noël received requests from various countries to sign his verses, which had been copied from the Bates' visitors' book:

No wand'ring nomad hesitates
To patronise the Quinta Bates
He finds it comfortable inside
And innocent of social pride.
He finds on entering the gate
An atmospheric opiate
The spirit of the place conserves
An anodyne for jangled nerves.
The water's hot, the beds are soft,
The meals are many a time and oft.
The flowers are sweet, the grass is green
The toilet is austerely clean,
Which, in this ancient continent,
Occasions vast astonishment.
The food is more than luxe enough
The cook not only cooks enough
But builds each afternoon for tea
A model of gastronomy.

The furniture is nicely placed
And signifies a catholic taste
The periods are slightly mixed
Some are between and some betwixt.

And now I feel it would be nice
In praising this small paradise
To mention with an awe profound
The one who makes the wheels go round.

Her name is plainly Mrs Bates
A strange capricious whim of Fate's
To crown with such banality
So great a personality.
Her friends who love the Quinta's fame
Disdain this unromantic name
And much prefer to call this dear,
Kind and enchanting person 'Tia'.
Though Tia is completely kind
She has a keen and lively mind
And when things seem too hard to bear
She'll soundly and robustly swear.
She's learned her life in Nature's school
And isn't anybody's fool.

Of every place I've been to yet
This I shall leave with most regret.

Refrain:

MAD ABOUT THE BOY

Mad about the boy!
I know it's stupid to be mad about
    the boy,
I'm so ashamed of 'it,
    But must admit
The sleepless nights I've had about
    the boy.

Walking down the street,
His eyes look out at me from people
    that I meet,
I can't believe it's true!
    But when I'm blue,
In some strange way I'm glad about
    the boy.

Lord knows I'm not a fool girl:
    I really shouldn't care;
Lord knows I'm not a school girl:
    In the flurry of her first affair.

If I could employ
    A little magic that would finally
    destroy
This dream that pains me,
    And enchains me,
But I can't, because I'm mad about
    the boy.

1. "The Boy's" Admirers

Prologue to the ninth number in " Words and Music" : The queue outside a cinema where one of the Boy's films is showing

3. *The Street-walker (Steffi Duna) adds her own love for-sale version of the refrain*

2. *The Lady (Joyce Barbour) Sings Her Infatuation*

The Lady, in her super-modern flat, confessing her secret passion over cocktails to her friend (Millie Sims), constitutes the first of the half-dozen episodes in this satire on film fans, in Noel Coward's brilliant revue at the Adelphi

"MAD ABOUT THE BOY

from "WORDS AND MUSIC"

NOEL COWARD

Words and Music by

Moderato

PIANO

I met him at a pa...
couple of years a-go, He was rather o-ver-heart-y, and ri...

HE BOY...

Noel Coward has scored yet another success in "Words and Music," at the Adelphi Theatre. In this very modern revue, satire tinged with pathos is the dominant note, and this is well exemplified on these two pages, where the song scena, "Mad About the Boy," in which the revolving-stage is used for quick changes of scene, is pictured. It has been said that the British public cannot appreciate satire. This is surely disproved by the fact that "Mad About the Boy" is one of the most popular numbers in the show

5. The Schoolgirl (Nora Howard) repeats the chorus with all the enthusiasm of a film-struck flapper

4. The Servant (Doris Hare) adds her quota to the prevailing madness

The Boy (Edward Underdown), his feet in hot water, deals cursorily with his adorers, via his Secretary (Cyril Butcher) and his Typist (Ann Codrington), while his Manicurist (Elizabeth Jenns) deals with his hands

6. The Boy Himself—at his "Fan-Mail"

"Send a photograph ... send a photograph ... send a photograph ..."

The long holiday ended at Colón, from whence Jeffery returned to England and where Noël, as great good luck would have it, found that the owner's suite in a freighter bound for Los Angeles was available. The ship was small and there were no other passengers; he could sunbathe wearing nothing at all, which he loved to do, on his own verandah. His streak of luck was running at the full, for on the very first morning out, just as he had hoped, the idea of a play for himself and the Lunts fell into his head. Writing virtually nude until six every evening, when he put on a pair of shorts for dinner, the play flowed easily and was finished and neatly typed two days before the ship docked at Los Angeles.

Noël's next venture, again a revue for Cochran, did not attain the same degree of success as *This Year Of Grace* three years before. Noël was now in a position to impose his ideas on Cochran and, in the event, mistakenly ignored the latter's warning that *Words And Music* lacked three of what he knew from experience were the essential ingredients for a revue – one or more star names, a team of brilliant designers, and fantastically good dancing. Even Mr Cochran's Young Ladies weren't given much to do except look lovely and sing the rather lugubrious *Children Of The Ritz*. Although the notices lavishly praised the revue and, to begin with, it showed every sign of being another Coward smash hit, Cochran in the end was proved right: business began to drop, it achieved a run of little more than five months and was the first Cochran-Coward production not to show a profit. There were two charmingly memorable songs – *Something To Do With Spring* and *The Party's Over Now* – but *Words And Music*'s chief claim to fame is that it introduced two of Noël's imperishables, *Mad About The Boy* and *Mad Dogs And Englishmen*.

The wild seeds of hope and ambition planted so long ago by Lynn Fontanne, Alfred Lunt and Noël came to ripe, cultivated fruition in *Design For Living* on 24 January 1933 at the Ethel Barrymore Theatre, New York. Three stars of such magnitude, equally matched in a well-nigh perfect vehicle, had seldom, if ever, been seen before, nor have they since. Lynn and Alfred were flawless comedians, their rapport and their quicksilver timing beyond compare. But, they had set themselves such a standard of perfection that they were seldom completely satisfied. Only very occasionally might one of them say, 'I think I was rather good tonight. I've got the breakfast scene right at last.' Usually it was, 'No, no Noëly [or Lynnie or Alfred], I was all over the place in the second act, I let you down badly. I *am* so sorry darling.' This self-denigration went on until Noël couldn't resist making fun of it and even wrote a skit about it which the trio performed for a charity benefit.

Lynn, Alfred and Noël in their old age loved to talk about the early days of their friendship, days long gone; it was known as 'going back to God knows when'. Lynn still clearly recalls the evening when she and Noël went to the first night of that famous farce *Getting Gertie's Garter* (Alfred was playing in *Clarence*, so it must be nearly sixty years ago). They were dressed to kill, made a star entrance to their seats up front, and everybody stared at them as they rolled about, aching with laughter, which was so loud that they infected the audience including the critics, and always took the credit for getting the play off to such a good start. Alfred, looking back on their long association, seemed only to remember how happy they had been, and Noël's kindness: 'I realize now how *kind* he always was to me. Surely he must have been angry with me sometimes, but I can't remember him ever showing it.' As a matter of fact, Noël was often angry with Alfred and showed it: he once attacked him with, 'What in God's name possessed you last night, playing that whole scene with a throb in your voice? Who do you think you are, the Habimah Players?' On being compared to the

Left: 'All that Luntery'; Noël, Alfred Lunt and Lynn Fontanne in New York at the time of their great Broadway success, Design For Living. *In London, a few years later, their roles were played by Rex Harrison, Diana Wynyard (below) and Anton Walbrook.*

"LOVE AMONG THE
ARTISTS"
REX HARRISON,
ANTON WALBROOK,
DIANA WYNYARD

Habimah Players (a renowned Hebrew company who played melodramas such as *The Dybbuk*), Alfred would laugh even in retrospect until he had to wipe away the tears. 'Oh, he was always so funny. And so kind', was all that he would admit to.

Lynn did not quite have the same ability to laugh at Noël, at least not in the early days. 'Was Noëly ever cross with you? Did he ever rebuke you?' she asked one of us. 'Yes, of course, often.' 'Well, I often came under fire when we were young and the strange thing was he never attacked me when I expected him to, when I felt perhaps I should have been ticked off. His attacks were usually utterly unexpected and often undeserved. It was very difficult to put up with, very hard to bear, and I sometimes wondered whether I could stand it. In the end, lying awake one night, the question came to me that I knew I had to answer honestly: *Can I manage without him for the rest of my life?* She smiled: 'The answer was quite simple. Of course I couldn't, and I loved him as he was, faults and all, from then on.'

A biography of the Lunts? Even Noël baulked at the impossibility.

It has been suggested many times that I should write their strange, loving story and on each occasion the subject came up my heart sank like a stone and I burst out into a kind of spiritual sweat. Not that anything I would say about them would ever be deprecating or unkind, but it must be remembered that they are magic creatures and magic creatures are vulnerable in different ways from ordinary mortals. As I would cheerfully plunge into a vat of boiling oil rather than hurt a hair of their heads, my pen will remain firmly sheathed. As one of the many nuns in *The Sound Of Music* remarked of Miss Mary Martin, 'How can you catch a moonbeam in your hand?' Catching a moonbeam in your hand would be falling off a log compared with catching and holding the truth about the Lunts between the covers of a book. Neither I nor anyone in this world could do it entirely successfully. Perhaps in some future existence Henry James, Anton Chekov and Sir James Barrie might have a bash at it, but I don't envy them the assignment.

Whenever Noël was in New York, which was often, he received an open-armed welcome at the legendary 'Round Table' in the Algonquin Hotel.

Reams have been written about the Round Table but no one seems to have remembered to mention what kind of food was ordered, or how and when it was consumed between the rallies of wit. Noël said that it was all rather catch-as-catch-can, the *great* thing to catch being a waiter's eye and then try to order above the hubbub; in his case Littleneck Clams followed by Eggs Benedict or anything that would 'slip down easy', accompanied in those days by an Old Fashioned or a Whiskey Sour. Although there was no guest list as such, and the number of persons present fluctuated from day to day, there was a sort of unspoken 'membership' without which an intruder would have been received with what was then known as the frozen mitt, and the Round Table therefore became what must have been the most concentrated daily gathering of wit in the history of America before or since. Alexander Woollcott seems to have been master of the lack of ceremony; friendship with him was an essential key to the entrée, which is why, because of her feuds with him, Edna Ferber's attendance was irregular. The regulars included Dorothy Parker, Robert Benchley, Harpo Marx, Alfred Lunt, Ben Hecht and Charles MacArthur, George Kaufman and his much-loved wife, Beatrice, and Marc Connelly; somewhat surprisingly the regal Kathleen Norris was an undoubted 'member' when she elected to appear. (Groucho Marx once happened upon the *grande-dame* novelist, clad in black satin with pearls, looking in a shop window on Fifth Avenue, approached her from the rear and goosed her. She turned on

Goldenhurst, Noël's Kent country home from the 1930s to the mid-1950s, was approached along a drive of poplar trees known to Lorn Loraine as Twig Avenue.

In the studio at Goldenhurst, Noël began to paint; here, too, he and Gertrude Lawrence began to rehearse the nine one-act plays that made up Tonight At 8.30.

him and in furious clarion tones cried, 'Not one more penny do you get! I've given you the best years of my life' – passers-by stopped in their tracks – 'and what have you given me in return you drunkard? *Nothing*! You have sucked me dry for twenty years!' Such a large crowd had gathered by the end of her long tirade that Groucho for once in his life retired defeated, and slunk away to more cries of 'Drunkard!' and 'Bloodsucker!' from Mrs Norris.)

Lynn Fontanne was also a regular at the Round Table when in New York and the reader may have noticed that she is not included in the foregoing list of wits: by her own admission she is not quick-witted (though she is mistress of the devastating remark from time to time) and, when we mentioned this to Adrianne Allen, she said, '*I* was always welcomed at the Round Table and I never opened my mouth!' We were rather taken aback by this and she continued, 'Don't be silly, I made a wonderful audience for them and they were all so busy being witty that they seldom had one!'

As well as their smart London houses, the more successful of the stage stars of the 1930s owned country estates in the counties nearest London. Noël, as we know, had Goldenhurst Farm in Kent and he was rightly proud of it and its one hundred and forty-nine acres, one hundred of which were let to a tenant farmer, so that, as well as being deafened by birdsong, as he put it, he and his guests were liable also to be wakened by the less musical bleating of sheep. The entrance to Goldenhurst, off the London-Dover road, was through a pretty wood bright with bluebells, primroses and wild cherry in the spring, after which came an avenue of poplars. Noël was

monarch of almost all he surveyed, for the house was built on a rise and at the seaward end of his property the land sloped away to the flatter lands of Romney Marsh, the Marsh so low-lying that the wide and distant view of the sea and the horizon often looked as though it were up in the sky. And on clear nights the long line of lights on the French coast glittered higher still.

The original farmhouse was sixteenth century and presumably so was the large, handsome barn, close by but separate. Noël soon linked the two by means of a long passage and built yet more guest rooms on the far side of the barn. Old tiles and bricks were used for these improvements, so that, from the outside, the effect was that of rambling and charmingly mellowed old age. In summer, the walls facing south to the lawn and gardens were blanketed with honeysuckle and climbing roses. Within, the same effect of age was maintained, though this had been achieved by that most modern and costly of interior decorators, Syrie Maugham, wife of Somerset Maugham, who had used soft colours almost throughout, beige and gentle greens predominating. Noël's friends, Jack Wilson, Gladys and David Herbert had had enormous fun rummaging through the antique shops dotted about the Marsh for chairs, sofas, pictures and Staffordshire china. Or attending auctions such as the one at Hurstmonceaux Castle from which they returned in triumph with a seven-foot-long carved overmantel by Grinling Gibbons, and a sensationally big pair of wings sprouting from an hourglass – *tempus fugit* – of Cornish tin, beaten and gilded: the latter was given the place of honour over the fireplace in the Big Room. Most of the foregoing, but especially the Grinling Gibbons and the wings, accompanied Noël in his changes of house for the rest of his life, even crossing the Atlantic and back, and are still in use today in his house in Switzerland.

Good neighbours were plentiful. Gladys Calthrop lived not far away in a converted old mill with the stream babbling through the drawing-room, and would come to stay for weekends or for weeks if need be when working with Noël on productions of such magnitude as *Bitter-Sweet* and *Cavalcade*. Noël's English publisher Alexander Frere and his wife Pat, daughter of Edgar Wallace, were special friends; intelligent, funny and kind, they lived in the same parish of Aldington. So did Erica Marx, who

Michael Arlen
Atalanta Arlen

Paris

W.C. Bushell
Amherst.

H.M.S. "Suffolk".
London.

Jill Olivier

London

Laurence Olivier

"

oct 4-6
London

Beatrice Lillie

Bobbie Andrews

Haymarket Theatre!

Gertrude Lawrence.

London.

Beatrice Eden

Alfred Lunt

Anthony Eden

Joyce Carey   Lynn Fontanne

Richard Addinsell

may or may not have been a collateral descendant of Karl Marx, but whenever he was given a generous helping of Iranian caviar by Erica, Noël enjoyed pretending it had been paid for out of the royalties from *Das Kapital*. Erica owned and herself ran the Hand and Flower Press in the village, turning out beautiful books, loyally including *The Art of Noël Coward* by Robert Greacen, when Noël's literary reputation was at its lowest ebb. Then there was Bob Boothby who emanated fun and laughter and was Noël's most vociferous political ally in their anger against Neville Chamberlain's policy during the years of appeasement leading to Munich and the Second World War.

Sir Philip Sassoon lived nearby at Lympne. One of his bonds with Noël was that it was he who brought T. E. Lawrence into Noël's life, for which Noël was forever grateful. Lawrence, himself a fine writer whom Noël admired, was unsparing in his praise of *Post Mortem* and especially of *Private Lives*, when it was being critically dismissed as merely entertaining and dangerously thin: he assured Noël that the writing, though spare, was strong and that *Private Lives* would live. The other bond was that Sir Philip was President of Lympne Flying Club and Noël Vice-President. An International Flying Rally was held each year with entries from all over Europe: a jolly event, climaxing in the presentation of the cups and prizes on the Saturday, after which all the pilots and, it seemed, most of the spectators – for there were always about two hundred people – trooped over for Noël's riotous party on the Goldenhurst lawn.

All through this period Noël enjoyed the peaks of theatrical and social success. The Goldenhurst visitors' book, now given to the Garrick Club

Below: Three of Noël's sixteen godchildren: Alan Williams (in 1935) with Emlyn and Molly and John Gielgud smiling happily; Daniel Massey (in 1933) with parents Raymond and Adrianne, and his nanny; and Hugo Morley (in 1968); others include Tarquin Olivier, David Niven Jr, Michael Attenborough, Juliet Mills and Caspar Fleming.

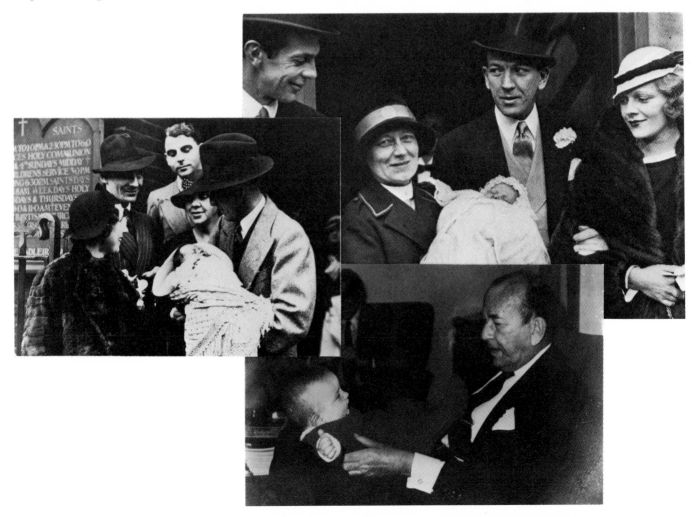

where it is on permanent display, bristles with illustrious names – Beatrice Lillie, Kreisler, Somerset Maugham, Laurence Olivier, Leslie Howard, Yvonne Printemps, Michael Arlen, Gladys Cooper, Emlyn Williams, Marie Tempest, the Duke of Kent and Princess Marina, Anthony Eden, John Gielgud, Prince Aly Khan, Rebecca West, and many other writers who are now not so famous, alas, as they were in their lifetimes: Sheila Kaye-Smith, G.B.Stern, Radclyffe Hall. The most regular visitor of all was, of course, Gertrude Lawrence.

Noël had by this time become equally celebrated on both sides of the Atlantic and the leading lights of the arts in America were his friends. One and all made a beeline for Goldenhurst, usually on their first weekend in England, some even driving straight from the docks after landing at Southampton. Or Noël would himself drive to meet them; his 'Al Capone' Rolls-Royce had by now been superseded by one originally built to Prince Aly Khan's specifications, in which he gloried. He was a good driver, though too fast for some of his passengers: a precious cargo of stars of both sexes would be given a carefree warning, 'Hold on to your hats, boys!' as they approached the bumps, familiar to Noël, on the country roads around Goldenhurst. Ina Claire and John Gilbert on their tempestuous honeymoon – came and behaved tempestuously; Joan Crawford and Douglas Fairbanks Jr spent some of the European part of theirs behaving as honeymooners should, and became Noël's dear friends for life. Then there were Fred Astaire, Gloria Swanson, Ruth Chatterton, Raymond Massey, Dorothy Gish, Grace Moore, Lynn and Alfred, Peggy Wood, Clifton Webb, Ruth Gordon, Helen Hayes and, inevitably, Elsa Maxwell (whom Noël called 'the Rose by any other Name-Dropper') transforming each of her visits into a party.

Mrs Alice Duer Miller (her most famous poem is *The White Cliffs Of Dover*) included among her talents mathematics as well as poetry, which fascinated Noël. 'When you get into the realm of higher mathematics', she explained, 'it *becomes* poetry.' Her and Noel's great crony Alexander

Post-Mortem, still professionally unproduced in England save on BBC television, did have one schoolboy production at Thame in 1966. A savage and bitter anti-war play, written in 1930, it was Noël's Journey's End.

Woollcott was blissfully happy at Goldenhurst, abusing Noël in shocking language whenever he was fiendishly clever on the croquet lawn or at the backgammon board, which was often – 'Bitch delivered of a drab!' being one of Mr Woollcott's more printable comments.

The range and number of Noël's friends was remarkable: nearly all the famous names just mentioned are those of people who became and remained dear to him and there were many more from *Who's Who In The Theatre* and Debrett to people in all walks of life all over the world. His gift for friendship was one more gift among his many, and it was to him an important one. Once truly given it was given for ever. His loyalty to his friends never wavered and his help in time of trouble never failed. He was much loved all his life and, as he wrote in his last poem, 'Happy am I who loved them so'.

Relaxation and jolly weekends apart, Goldenhurst was for Noël a refuge and a retreat, and he would race there by car or train whenever he could. The pattern varied according to his occupation of the moment. If he was acting, he always drove down on the Saturday night after the second performance, however late, even if he had had to go to a supper-party. He would be back in Gerald Road in time for tea and a rest on the Monday (he had the knack of being able to snatch some sleep at will for a given time) before facing the play that night. If he was writing or composing, the routine differed: he quite simply went to Goldenhurst and stayed there until the job was finished. In contrast to sleeping late after acting the night before, he loved, when writing, to be called early, at half past six – 'the morning's my best time' – and, after a good breakfast of eggs and bacon or two pork sausages, he could be at work by half past seven. He wrote at a

big scrubbed oak table facing the panoramic view, unlike most writers (Mr Maugham was quite shocked and advised him to face the wall). If composing, he, of course, worked at a piano, 'his' one of the two grand pianos in the enormous drawing room: two, as at Gerald Road, because he delighted in playing double piano with other composers or musicians who happened to be visiting, such as Richard Rodgers, Richard Addinsell or Kay Thompson, who could provide him with a challenge in exciting improvisation.

Noël's mother, father and his 'dear little Auntie Vida' lived together in the old part of the house, seldom harmoniously: in fact, dual or triple pitched battles were frequent between them. He had to listen to all three accounts of their quarrels soon after arrival, no matter how late; at two or even three in the morning a light could still be seen burning in his mother's window and so, exhausted as he was at the end of a crowded week in London, he knew it was imperative to climb the stairs to see her, so that she could be the first to get in with her version of the latest domestic drama. Next morning Noël would firmly tell all three of them, separately or together, to 'shut up and let me get on with my work', which he then, equally firmly, proceeded to do in his own tranquil quarters far away at the other end of the house.

'From the moment the curtain went up on the young Yvonne Printemps sitting up in a pink bed singing *J'ai Deux Amants* in *L'Amour Masqué*, she annihilated in me any critical faculty', Noël wrote. Later on, when playing with her, he admitted that she could, very rarely, become just a shade too much the coy, cute French coquette, but he continued: 'In common with

Below and overleaf: 'For Noël with love': Yvonne Printemps, star of his 1934 Conversation Piece *and therefore the first to sing* I'll Follow My Secret Heart. *Noël himself played the male lead, uneasily, and was soon replaced by Mlle Printemps' husband, Pierre Fresnay.*

CHARLES B. COCHRAN
presents
YVONNE PRINTEMPS
in
CONVERSATION PIECE
A Play with Music
BY
NOEL COWARD
THE PLAY DIRECTED BY THE AUTHOR

CHAPPELL & CO, LTD
50, NEW BOND ST.
LONDON, W.1
NEW YORK & SYDNEY
CHAPPELL S.A.
PARIS

PRINTED IN ENGLAND

I'LL FOLLOW MY SECRET HEART	2/- NET
NEVERMORE	2/- "
REGENCY RAKES	2/- "
THERE'S ALWAYS SOMETHING FISHY ABOUT THE FRENCH	2/- "
VALSE (PIANO SOLO)	2/- "
PIANO SELECTION	2/6 "

thousands of others I thought that she could do no wrong; she was lovely to look at, her nose delightfully *retroussée*; her voice beyond comparison with anybody else's – liquid nightingale is perhaps the nearest one can get – and she possessed the very essence of star quality, triple-distilled.' In the years that followed, Noël went to Paris to hear Yvonne in everything she did: *Mozart, Mariette, Trois Valses* and the rest. In addition to her alluring appearance – clothes by Lanvin, ropes of pearls, and two tiny lapdogs tinkling with tinier bells – she was unexpectedly funny and jolly: after supper in a restaurant and one or two whiskies she would think nothing while still at the table of singing an aria from *Madame Butterfly* right through at the top of her voice out of sheer *joie de vivre*, whether anyone listened to her or not – but they usually listened.

It was inevitable that Noël should dream of writing an operette for her one fine day, and in 1933 he wrote *Conversation Piece* with her and her voice in mind. To his joy she accepted and appeared in it in London, singing in English for the first and only time – if English it can be called, for she never mastered the language; but no matter, the sounds she made were exquisite. 'It was a big occasion', W. A. Darlington wrote in the *Telegraph*, 'and became a great one as soon as Yvonne Printemps appeared . . . When the end came and she took a call alone, the warmth and volume of applause moved her visibly to the verge of tears. . . . It was from the moment when she first sang the romantic theme-song, *I'll Follow My Secret Heart*, that she had her audience enthralled last night. Mr Coward shares her triumph or rather, since he is author, composer, producer and chief male actor in this brilliant show, he enjoys a separate triumph all to himself.'

Not long after this Noël, encouraged by Jack, made the (for him) momentous decision to leave Mr Cochran and his management and to form

Opposite and following: the extensive coverage of Private Lives, *1930.*

Operette, *1938. Despite* The Stately Homes of England, Dearest Love, Where Are The Songs We Sung? *and the work of a large cast headed by Fritzi Massary, Irene Vanbrugh and Griffith Jones, the show was not a success.*
Overleaf: Portrait of Noël by Clemence Dane.

THE PLAY

PICTORIAL

With which are incorporated "THE PLAY" "THE PLAY SOUVENIR." "THE STAGE SOUVENIR."

"PRIVATE LIVES"

No. 344

VOL. LVII

1 S. NET

MONTHLY

NOEL COWARD

GERTRUDE LAWRENCE

"Private Lives"

By Noel Coward.

Sybil Chase .... Adrianne Allen
Elyot Chase .... Noel Coward
Victor Prynne .... Laurence Olivier
Amanda Prynne .... Gertrude Lawrence
Louise (a Maid) .... Everley Gregg

AMANDA and Elyot are the fine, flippant flower of Mr. Coward's talent. What would happen if the parts were indifferently well played we tremble to think, but Miss Gertrude Lawrence has a brilliant sparkle and an extraordinary skill in embellishing speech with silence, Mr. Coward's wayward mannerisms have here their most fitting background, and the dialogue which might seem in print a trickle of inanities becomes in the theatre a perfectly timed and directed interplay of nonsense.

There are moments when even Mr. Coward falters. Before the quarrel reaches its climax the play, because there is nothing else to happen and the author's patter is exhausted, is temporarily converted into a concert party; and again, before breakfast, the patter nearly peters out. But Mr. Coward can pad as no one else can pad ; he has made of dramatic upholstery an art and provides a delightful support for our utmost laziness. Some day, perhaps, he will invite us to more austere pleasure ; we must be content to await the passing of his determination to be defiantly young. "Let's be superficial and pity the poor Philosophers," says Elyot in a moment of solemnity. "Let's blow trumpets and squeakers and enjoy the party as much as we can. . . . Come and kiss me, darling, before your body rots, and worms pop in and out of your eye sockets." If there were people who spoke like that about the time of the Peace of Versailles, have they not since grown up?—*The Times.*

Do people of apparent birth and breeding really do these things? The sort of things, I mean, that they do in "Private Lives," Mr. Noel Coward's new comedy, presented by Mr. Charles B. Cochran at the new Phœnix Theatre last night before what is commonly called a brilliant audience. The brilliant audience laughed and applauded all right, though that may have been due to the often extremely witty dialogue, as well as some very excellent acting—but the question still persists ; and with a corollary to it.

Apart from this man *v.* woman smacking business—which may be authentic in some sort of real life, but is not remarkably attractive on the stage—the piece contains much that is amusing, but the halt and slow-down after the first act is marked. The acting last night, however, was of a high standard throughout ; Mr. Coward and Miss Gertrude Lawrence (acting, I believe, her first "straight" part) played the (first) husband and wife in just the right key of comedy—and if the scrap was inevitable, they certainly scrapped with agility, and even some degree of grace. Mr. Laurence Olivier and Miss Adrianne Allen, in their rather thankless parts as second-edition spouses, gave them admirable support, though they scrapped less interestingly ; Miss Lawrence's frocks were charming.—*Daily Telegraph.*

Noel Coward is the play-boy of the London stage. He has raised flippancy to the plane of genius, and in his new "intimate comedy," which delighted the audience at the opening of the Phœnix Theatre last night, he even champions flippancy as the only wise treatment of life.

I for one will not quarrel with him, especially as in this new play he rather pathetically shows that his flippancy hides a sense of tragedy.

But first of all I should like to praise the decoration of this new playhouse. It is a theatre and not a cubist cave of mysteries. The warm scheme of colour makes it one of the prettiest theatres in London. It is cosy, intimate and inspiriting.

A quick-witted audience, inured to Noel Cowardism, also helped in the success of "Private Lives." What would happen if his witticisms missed fire? They will hardly bear the cold test of print.

Gertrude Lawrence, as the first wife, was a revelation to those who have only seen her in revue. The scene in which she and Noel Coward, each of whom is supposed to have re-married, meet at the French hotel on their respective honeymoons was acted with a lightness and a reality which one seldom sees on the London stage.

Some of the best comedy in this amusing play comes at the very end, when the two wives and their husbands have morning coffee after a night of wreckage. I did not quite understand why Adrianne Allen, as the second wife, and Laurence Olivier, as the second husband, should have started a slanging match, for they are not in love, but it enabled Gertrude Lawrence and Noel Coward to slip away with their bags to begin their love and quarrels all over again.—*News Chronicle.*

A triumphant return for Miss Gertrude Lawrence and Mr. Noel Coward, coupled with the opening last night of Mr. Sidney Bernstein's beautiful new Phœnix Theatre, and Mr. C. B. Cochran's presentation of Mr. Noel Coward's own new "intimate comedy," "Private Lives," could not help but make a brilliant occasion.

There was more than this—an evening full of cleverness and characteristically daring trivialities on Mr. Coward's part, with Miss Lawrence proving herself an actress possessed of an armoury of delicate accomplishments for comedy of this kind that she had simply no reason to reveal before.

She has achieved that perfect poise and grace that makes it possible for her to be doing nothing or anything and to be charming always. She can use a poignant voice in saying it is a fine day or asking for a cigarette which suggests vistas of personality. She has created, too, apparently specially for this play, a faculty of suddenly flaming out into a pretty passion—in short, that blessed thing called temperament.

As to the play, it is certainly a masterpiece in its own kind of easy-going inconsequence. It has any number of witty, acid lines, a wonderful duologue of fifty minutes, and two other little scenes that are really much better pieces of work.

As an actor, Mr. Coward is entirely at ease and self-possessed, speaks his own lines with a quiet incisiveness no one else could give them, and plays up to Miss Lawrence with complete understanding. One cannot say, however, that he creates a lovable character out of Elyot—represented as a disillusioned, aimless wanderer through life, believing in nothing, hoping for nothing, caring for nothing. Still it is, presumably, the study of a typical modern "private life," and as such is to be accepted.—*Morning Post.*

AMANDA: "Whose yacht is that?"
ELYOT: "The Duke of Westminster's, I expect. It
always is."
AMANDA: "I wish I were on it."
ELYOT: "I wish you were, too."
AMANDA: "There's no need to be nasty."

ELYOT: "You're looking very lovely, you know, in this damned moonlight; your skin is clear and cool, and your eyes are shining, and you're growing lovelier and lovelier every second, as I look at you. You don't hold any mystery for me, darling, do you mind? There isn't a particle of you that I don't know, and remember, and want."

AMANDA: "I'm glad, my sweet."

ELYOT: "More than any desire anywhere, deep down in my deepest heart I want you back again—please———"

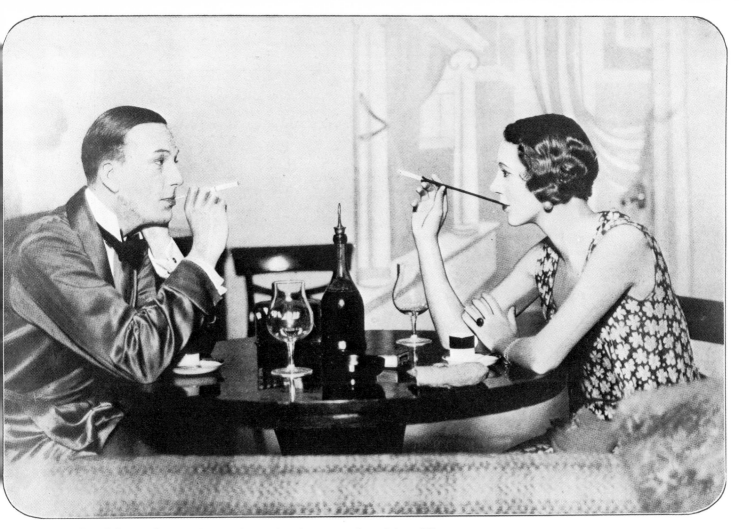

With Coward and Gertrude Lawrence, then at the height of their stage alliance, were Adrianne Allen and Laurence Olivier. *Private Lives opened London's new Phoenix Theatre but (such was Noël's* determination not to bore himself by a long run) *played only three months there and three months on Broadway. Since 1930 not a year has passed without some sort of revival somewhere in the world.*

SOMEDAY I'LL FIND YOU

from
"PRIVATE LIVES"

Words and Music by   NOËL COWARD

THEY JAZZ
And all is peace and joy

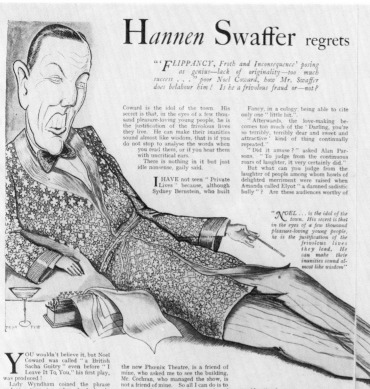

Hannen Swaffer regrets that "Noel Coward-ice"

"'FLIPPANCY, Froth and Inconsequence' posing as genius—lack of originality—too much success . . ." poor Noel Coward, how Mr. Swaffer does belabour him! Is he a frivolous fraud or—not?

in the Theatre has provided the Bright Young Few with a new form of Idolatry

"THE followers he attracts are nearly all know-nothings. They do not stimulate his brain."

Coward is the idol of the town. His secret is that, in the eyes of a few thousand pleasure-loving young people, he is the justification of the frivolous lives they live. He can make their inanities sound almost like wisdom, that is if you do not stop to analyse the words when you read them, or if you hear them with uncritical ears.

There is nothing in it but just idle nonsense, gaily said.

I HAVE not seen "Private Lives" because, although Sydney Bernstein, who built

"NOEL . . . is the idol of the town. His secret is that in the eyes of a few thousand pleasure-loving young people, he is the justification of the frivolous lives they lead. He can make their inanities sound almost like wisdom."

YOU wouldn't believe it, but Noel Coward was called "a British Sacha Guitry" even before "I Leave It To You," his first play, was produced!

Lady Wyndham coined the phrase and at a time, too, when she had only read, and not seen, this youthful effort, which was produced before Noel was twenty-one, so that someone else had to sign the contract!

"I feel that Mr. Coward will be a notable recruit to the ranks of our native dramatists," said Lady Wyndham, "and I am happy to introduce his work to London."

Well, much has happened in the ten years which have passed since then. Lady Wyndham has been absolutely justified, for Noel Coward's work, much as I have criticised it, resembles closely the work of Sacha Guitry, for, like that French Jew, Noel is a dramatist, an actor, a stage director and an expert in putting on the boards flippancy, froth and inconsequence, so expertly shimmered that, trifling as it is, it looks like genius—that is when Noel himself takes an active part in the production.

Yet it is not for that reason that Noel

the new Phoenix Theatre, is a friend of mine, who asked me to see the building, Mr. Cochran, who managed the show, is not a friend of mine. So all I can do is to turn on the gramophone records of "Private Lives" and judge it from them.

It is fair because, no doubt, in choosing extracts, the best ones were taken. Yet I am still wondering why, while one critic said, "You will have to be very modern and bright if you are to enjoy Noel Coward's new comedy"—this one quoted from the play a woman's remark, "I cannot find my lipstick," and the man's reply, "Send down to the kitchen for some cochineal"—another one said, "The best play of the year and the most amusing for many years."

I turn to the criticism of "Private Lives" written by Alan Parsons, and find that, while he says that "such a tale is not meant to instruct, to improve or to uplift, the only questions then are, 'Does it move one, and does it amuse?' Well, the little bit of love-making in the first act was played with such delicacy and feeling and such reticence that it certainly did move one."

Fancy, in a eulogy, being able to cite only one "little bit."

"Afterwards, the love-making becomes too much of the 'Darling, you're so terribly, terribly dear and sweet and attractive' kind of thing continually repeated."

"Did it amuse?" asked Alan Parsons. "To judge from the continuous roars of laughter, it very certainly did."

But what can you judge from the laughter of people among whom howls of delighted merriment were raised when Amanda called Elyot "a damned sadistic bully"? Are these audiences worthy of

consideration?

"I prefer to dwell on the more spontaneous and typical Coward wit," goes on Parsons, trying to make out a case.

"Whose yacht is that?" he quotes, going on to print the reply: "The Duke of Westminster's, I expect. It always is."

"I could never tire of that kind of thing," he comments, "and I am glad to say there is much more like that."

Now I am very fond of Alan Parsons, whose brain I admire, but, frankly, I do not consider a "witticism" like this any more than a casual remark, heard probably at some dinner table and then written down so that silly people might think it bright.

Foes though we may seem, my relations with Noel Coward have always been of a friendly kind. I admire his quick brain, his charm of manner, his kindliness to lots of people, and his modesty, which is such that Walter Hackett told me recently that, when he went to a lunch given in celebration of Pinero's seventieth birth-

day, Noel Coward, then at the height of his success, was almost the most modest man in the room.

What I deplore in him is that a young man so clever and so industrious is wasted on a stage which, at this moment, requires great courage of thought and great originality.

UNFORTUNATELY, Noel Coward has not got an original mind. It would seem that he goes to dinner-table conversations for his dialogue—they always sound like that, even if it is not so—whereas his plots too nearly resemble those which have been used with greater effect by other people.

"Bitter Sweet," which I thought would run for four months, made my judgment seem, for once, ridiculous. It has run for well over a year, to packed houses. I thought it would be killed by the vulgar scene in which four he-he young men were shown posturing and posing, and by a quartette of "ladies of

the town" who, I thought, would certainly frighten away family audiences.

"If the Coward show is to have a wide appeal," I said, "several things must come out."

For once they did not come out. Yet the show ran on. . . .

We have to face the fact that there are in London to-day a small crowd of silly young people, whose doings are chronicled as though they were important, who advertise each other, and boost each other, and make a lot of feeble noise. All these young know-nothings, think-nothings, do-nothings rush in the train of

Noel Coward, who, as he stands far above them in ambition, in endeavour and in achievement, is a sort of god whom they worship. They blah and they bleat so loudly that some foolish people are apt to interpret it as the opinion of London.

Noel Coward, unfortunately, has been too successful. He is like Seymour Hicks in the sense that he found it too easy to do things. He can take an idea, polish it up, apparently, in a few days, and, although it is only imitation, he often makes it look like real jewellery.

There is no phrase that you can take out of any one of his plays. There is not one original thought to which you can point.

Yet he has become so skilled that even E. A. Baughan, writing for the Nonconformist "Daily News," calls his new play, "Private Lives," genius, although I am afraid the ultra-modernity of its attitude towards life would so much shock their ideas that I hope readers of the "Daily News" never go to see the play.

I can only judge it from the gramophone record from which I copied down the following extracts.—

Noel: "Would you be young always—if you could choose?"

Gertrude: "No, I don't think so, no: if it meant having those awful bull's-glands popped into one."

Noel: "Cow's for you, dear. Bull's for me."

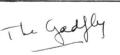

Decorations by TOM TITT

Gertrude: "We certainly live in a marvellous age. It must be so horrible for the poor animals being experimented on."

Noel: "Not when the experiment is successful. Why, in Vienna, I believe, you can see whole lines of decrepit, old rats carrying on like the Filler girls."

Gertrude: "Oh, darling!"

Now, all serious-minded men and women must deplore the Voronoff idea that, for sex gratification, old men and women may be made young again by grafting glands. Noel talks about this quite flippantly. He has nothing to say of it that is new. He merely treats vivisection as a silly jest, whereas humanitarians know that most vivisection experiments are a waste of time that results only in the needless torturing of animals.

If there is a case for vivisection, let some dramatist put it seriously. It is certainly not something to joke about, whether you are an animal or not.

SINCE his last success, "Bitter Sweet," Noel has been round the world. You would have thought he would have had something to say. Yet this is all, apparently, to judge from the record, that he seems called upon to remark upon something the romance *(Continued on p. 112.)*

(Continued on p. 112.)

"ALL these young know-nothings, do-nothings, rush in the train of Noel Coward, who, far above them in ambition, in endeavour and in achievement, is a sort of God, whom they worship. They blah and bleat so loudly that some foolish people are apt to interpret it as the opinion of London."

Hannen Swaffer, still unimpressed by Noël's theory that 'the primary function of the theatre is to amuse, not to reform, improve or edify people'. Writers in The Gadfly *appear to agree.*

SUZY PRIM

…nfants, pardon, les amants terribles …nt il s'agit, pouvant être de tous les …ys.

Daniel et Annette ont divorcé. Daniel …remarie avec Lucie et Annette avec …ctor. Grâce au hasard, dieu des poli… …rs et des dramaturges, les deux cou… …s, au premier jour de leur seconde …e de mie!, descendent dans le même …ce, occupent des appartements mi… …ns ouvrant sur la…

Left: Coward and Lawrence together on Broadway, as they were to be on only one other occasion; Someday I'll Find You *was the song from the play, and* Les Amants Terribles *was* Private Lives *in French.*

The Gadfly

20

On Saturday, September 20th, the Doctor and I went to the King's Theatre to see "Private Lives," "an intimate comedy by Noel Coward."

What a pity such lives cannot be kept **private**!

The play, with the exception of a certain amount of smart back chat, consisted of large buckets of stable manure thrown all over the great audience for over two hours.

The four degenerates (I am speaking of the characters assumed) laughed and jeered at truth, honour, life, love, marriage, sin and death.

It was a disgusting exhibition of moral and social decadence, (imagine the execrable taste of making a joke about a still-born child.)

Of course these four players in their own private lives may be quite moral and respectable. I know nothing about them and don't want to.

But, apart from box office receipts, what kind of effect, other than one wholly bad, can be produced in the minds of many thousands of people who saw this play?

Twenty years ago such a production would have been impossible.

Perhaps the saddest feature about it was the way in which it was received.

Hundreds and hundreds of apparently quite moral and respectable people also laughed at truth, honour, life, love, marriage, sin and death.

May I suggest to them that it is only a very short step from laughing at what is wrong to doing what is wrong?

On leaving the theatre I saw Mr. Parker Thomas in the crush.

I said, "What do you think of it?"

He said, "Rotten."

It was a complete summary of the evening's degradation.

And now London is to be afflicted with this filth.

his own company, Transatlantic Productions, consisting of himself, Jack, Lynn and Alfred. Financially this may have been a good move, but there is no doubt that without Cochran's guiding hand and wise advice, and with himself in complete control, not one of Noël's musicals – although they always gave much pleasure to his own special public – ever really succeeded from then on. His next essay in the genre, *Operette*, in 1938 is a good example of this: the score includes some lovely songs (though with rather melancholy lyrics) as well as the show-stopping *Stately Homes Of England* and it did introduce Fritzi Massary, magnetic star of the great days of operette in Berlin and Vienna, to London audiences who loved her; but the book was weak to the point of insignificance and *Operette* was one of the least successful musical plays Noël ever wrote.

Transatlantic Productions – the title was not used: 'John C. Wilson presents' replacing it on the bills – got off to a disastrous start with Sam Behrman's *Biography*, in which the sparkling Ina Claire failed to repeat her New York success, despite Noël's direction and Laurence Olivier as leading man. Perhaps Noël's name on the posters helped to give the impression that the comedy was 'lukewarm Coward'; in any event, by the end of the first week the cast were on half salaries and *Biography* ground to a halt after a few more weeks.

Their next venture was, however, an out and out success from all points of view. Noël and Gertie opened in *Tonight At 8.30* in January 1936, together again at 'their' theatre, the Phoenix, acting, singing and dancing with more charm, chic and allure than ever in nine one-act plays of wide diversity, a triple bill being given at each of three performances in succession. *Tonight At 8.30* was without doubt the supreme display of Noël's versatility within the bounds of one production, as author, actor and director nine times over, often singing and dancing into the bargain.

Tonight At 8.30, *1936: the most ambitious and complex of all Noël's legitimate theatre projects, and both the climax and the end of his partnership with Gertrude Lawrence.* Shadow Play, Ways and Means *and* Family Album *were just three of the nine plays acted on alternate nights in* Tonight At 8.30. Brief Encounter *started here (as* Still Life*) and the score included,* Play, Orchestra, Play *and the* Red Peppers *music-hall pastiches.*

Coward Contrasts

A Worm in Rebellion in Balham :
A Romantic Reunion in Mayfair

"SHADOW PLAY" and *Fumed Oak* are two of the second trilogy of plays in the *Coward To-night* at 8.30 repertoire at the Phœnix. Both of them have Noel Coward and Gertrude Lawrence as a husband - and - wife combination, but there the likeness ends. *Shadow Play* is a gentle sentimental trifle about an unhappy young wife who in a sleeping - draught dream finds her way back to her honeymoon mood, and leads her husband by the same road with her sleepily delirious talk. They sing a little and dance a little, and the end is a happy-ever-after one. By complete contrast, *Fumed Oak* is a low - life variation on Maugham's *Bread-winner* theme of domestic rebellion. Coward's downtrodden husband, whose £500 of savings give him courage for revolt and flight, is a gloriously unexpected piece of writing and acting, a very worm of worms, brilliantly described and interpreted. Gertrude Lawrence, with the thoroughness of her versatile genius, turns herself into Doris Gow, the slatternly nagging wife

Below : Fumed 'Oak—"*It'll have to be a very little piece of your mind—you can't afford much*"

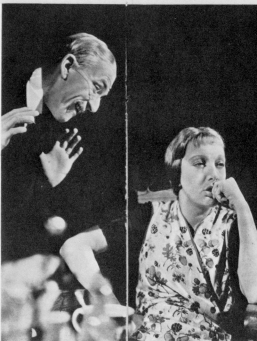

"*Cold ham—what a surprise*"

Right : "*I think Elsie's awful*"

Shadow Play—"*It'll be all right now, I promise*"
Noel Coward and Gertrude Lawrence as the Young Marrieds who find they are still in love

"*I could never love anybody else that much—but you*"

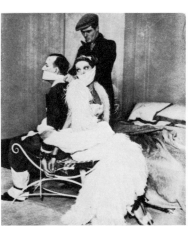

At one otherwise run-of-the-mill matinée towards the end of the run, cast and audience alike were startled to see an elderly gentleman standing on his seat, applauding loudly and shouting 'Bravo!' during the curtain calls. It was Sir Seymour Hicks, who then went round to see Noël and said, 'The time has come for me to give you Edmund Kean's sword. I've often wondered who it should be handed on to – now I know.' And next morning the sword, with Kean's signature inscribed on the scabbard, was delivered to Noël at Gerald Road. The sword had been handed down via Irving, who had been given it by an old character actor from Kean's company out of gratitude for being given work by Irving when he was destitute. Irving, in turn, gave it to William Terris, his handsome young leading man, who was stabbed to death when entering the Adelphi stage door on 16 December 1897 (two years to the day before Noël was born), whereupon it became the property of his daughter Ellaline, the pretty, smiling star of musical comedy, and her husband, Seymour Hicks, who jointly decided that Noël was worthy of it.

Twenty years or so later Noël was beginning to worry as to whom he, in his turn, should give the sword – who was 'the most promising young actor'? The problem for Noël was not so easy to solve as it had been for Sir Seymour: by this time his contemporaries had already been knighted and crowned with laurels, but among the younger generation several potentially great actors – Richard Burton, Peter O'Toole, Albert Finney – had burst upon the scene to everyone's delight and had then, perhaps wisely, deserted it for films and television. In the end he bequeathed it to the National Theatre Museum, which, soon after his death, became a dream never to be realized. The sword will now go to the Theatre Museum and in the meantime is safe in the good hands of Lord Olivier.

Present Indicative, Noël's first volume of autobiography, was published in 1937 and was widely read, admired and enjoyed in all English-speaking countries. But acclaim from the more 'intellectual' critics was denied Noël, as it always had been and always would be. After dismissing the book as 'almost always shallow and often dull', Cyril Connolly wrote:

Noël and Gertie in New York at the end of the 1930s and of their remarkable thirty-year partnership.

What are we left with? The picture, carefully incomplete, of a success; probably of one of the most talented and prodigiously successful people the world has ever known – a person of infinite charm and adaptability whose very adaptability, however, makes him inferior to a more compact and worldly competitor in his own sphere, like Cole Porter; and an essentially unhappy man, a man who gives one the impression of having seldom really thought or really lived and is intelligent enough to know it. But what can he do about it? He is not religious, politics bore him, art means facility or else brickbats, love wild excitement and the nervous breakdown. There is only success, more and more of it, till from his pinnacle he can look down to where Ivor Novello and Beverley Nichols gather samphire on a ledge, and to where, a pinpoint on the sands below, Mr Godfrey Winn is counting pebbles. But success is all there is, and that even is temporary. For one can't read any of Noël Coward's plays now ... they are written in the most topical and perishable way imaginable, the cream in them turns sour overnight – they are even dead before they are turned into talkies, however engaging they may seem at the time. This book reveals a terrible predicament, that of a young man with the Midas touch, with a gift that does not creep and branch and flower, but which turns everything it touches into immediate gold. And the gold melts, too.

This attack, which Noël thought verged on the venomous and was innaccurate to the point of silliness, nevertheless upset him deeply and genuinely puzzled him. There is no denying that at this point in his life he would have loved to have been praised by the intellectuals rather than to

NOEL COWARD HOST TO
THE DUCHESS OF KENT

As President of the Actor's Orphanage, Noël enjoyed the challenge of organizing the annual Theatrical Garden Party, which Princess Marina, Duchess of Kent, attended in 1937 (far left).

Above, two photos by Noël: Princess Marina with Princess Alexandra, and Prince George, Duke of Kent, practising wearing his bearskin for the Trooping the Colour.

Court Dress

Mr. Noel Coward, neat as a new pin in his Court dress, was just leaving his house in Gerald Street for the Levée at St. James's Palace

With Best wishes for Xmas, 1940.

receive their pity and contempt, but Mr Connolly seemed to be writing with condescension from a pinnacle even higher than that on which he had placed Noël. Who had placed *him* there, Noël wanted to know? Himself? Was there a hint of jealousy induced by the universal popularity and success enjoyed by Noël but withheld from Connolly? And why was it withheld from him if he was so clever and omniscient? Although they managed an uneasy acquaintance whenever they met socially in later years, Noël never really forgave or forgot Mr Connolly's gratuitous attack, but with the passing of time it fell into its place along with others of the same kind. Noël wrote at the end of his life: 'Oh how fortunate I was to have been born poor. If Mother had been able to send me to private school, Eton and Oxford or Cambridge, it would probably have set me back years. I have always distrusted too much education and intellectualism [this was written after a surfeit of reading Lytton Strachey and other Bloomsberries]. It seems to me that they are always dead wrong about things that really matter.' And *Present Indicative* is still in print and being bought today, more than forty years later.

Among the other things about which Cyril Connolly was wrong was Noël's boredom with politics: he was at that time and for the next decade about as involved with politics and politicians as it was possible for any layman to be.

Into the 1940s, alone.

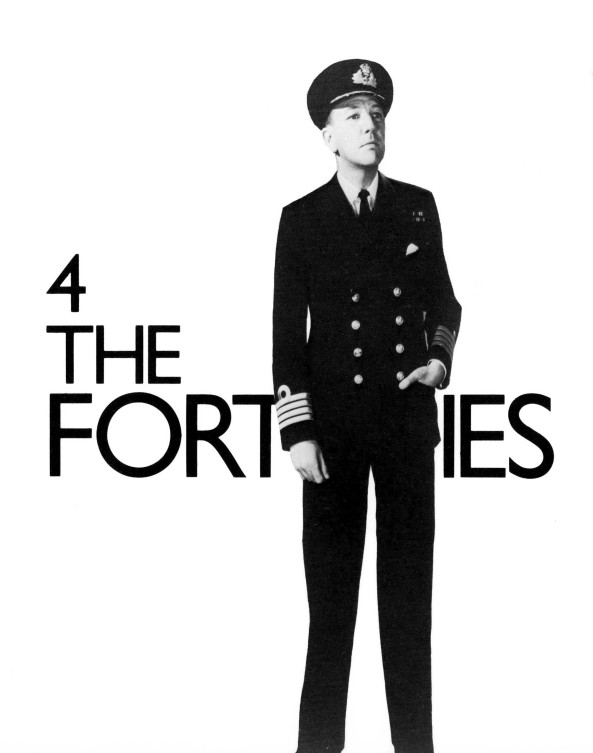

4
THE
FORTIES

THE THUNDERCLOUD OF AN INEVITABLE WAR WITH GERMANY threatened from the otherwise clear skies of the late 1930s – clear as far as most people were concerned, that is. There was an atmosphere of gaiety, of trying to make hay while the sun still shone – 'nothing to worry about except the destruction of civilization', Noël wrote. He became more and more conscious of the folly of the Government's policy of appeasement, and increasingly angered by it. Politically, he had never in his life felt more strongly about any other issue. He was, of course, not alone in this, but his violent views were those of a minority; nonetheless, he was not afraid to speak his mind loudly and clearly at every opportunity, until even some of his closest friends told him to his face that he had become a bore on the subject or called him a war-monger. But he continued, convinced of the imminence of war and of chaos and destruction, and his views inevitably brought him closer in sympathy with those of like mind. These happened to be men in high office, most of them of Cabinet rank: Anthony Eden, Duff Cooper, and his old friends Robert Vansittart and George Lloyd, the two latter perhaps being the most vehement, because they added their open dislike of Germany and the Germans to their distrust of appeasement. Noël was, therefore, extremely well informed throughout the ominous years leading up to Munich and on to the outbreak of war itself. He also felt an increasing awareness of what it meant to be English, and out of this feeling came an urge to write the patriotic *This Happy Breed* in the early summer of 1939. He also wrote *Present Laughter*, the most autobiographical of all his plays. Rehearsals of these two plays were due to begin in August and, before starting work, he decided to spend a long holiday taking what might possibly be, and was, one last long look at eastern Europe. He visited Poland, Russia, Finland and Scandinavia to get the political 'feel' of them, which gave rise to the suspicion that clung to Noël in the coming years that he was a spy for the British Government. Lawrence Durrell, then stationed in Danzig, reported that during Noël's visit to that city German agents, already suspicious, became convinced that Noël was a British agent; which was probably why his name was included on the famous Nazi Black List of those who were to be exterminated when Germany won the war. After V.E. Day, when the Black List was published, he received a telegram from Rebecca West: MY DEAR THE PEOPLE WE SHOULD HAVE BEEN SEEN DEAD WITH!

Bob Boothby's country house was near Goldenhurst; he and Noël were cronies anyway, visiting each other with their house-guests most weekends, and they became even closer in the years before the war, laughing their heads off at almost everything. Even the target of their contempt and hatred, Neville Chamberlain, could become the object of their ridicule. Bob (later Lord) Boothby, like the aforementioned kindred spirits, was in a position to give Noël the latest 'inside' parliamentary news and he it was who shed light on a mysterious telephone call Noël received one morning that August from Sir Campbell Stuart, whom Noël had never heard of, but who said that he must see him urgently late that very evening and asked if Noël liked Paris. Bob laughed at Noël's ignorance, when he arrived for luncheon, and explained that Sir Campbell's was indeed a name to reckon with and that he was obviously going to ask him to set up an

Bob Boothby and Godfrey Winn at Goldenhurst in happier times.

organization (later described by Bob as 'ridiculous') to work for British propaganda in Paris. Noël was hoping that his job for the duration would somehow be in connection with the Navy, and, as Bob was dining that evening with Winston Churchill at Chartwell, he kindly arranged that Noël should come with him and ask Churchill's advice. His advice was not at all to Noël's liking: in a nutshell it was that Noël should 'go out and sing *Mad Dogs And Englishmen* when the guns are firing – that's your job!' He was to be proved right two years later, but meanwhile Sir Campbell, a tall thin figure in black, materialized as promised at midnight at Gerald Road and outlined his plan for Noël to go to Paris in the event of war to make friendly liaison with the French Commissariat d'Information. Noël made an attempt to wriggle out by going next morning to the Foreign Office to ask Sir Robert Vansittart for a second opinion, but was advised to accept, and so the die was cast.

Noël, Joyce Carey, Leonora Corbett and the rest of the company pressed on gallantly with rehearsals of *Present Laughter* and *This Happy Breed* until the Germans invaded Poland on Friday 1 September, when plans were shelved. Two days later, Chamberlain made his lugubrious announcement of the outbreak of war and four days after that Noël was ordered to fly to Paris. He had been chosen for the post because it was felt that propaganda should be a job for a writer and that the British should provide someone of an eminence equal to his French counterparts, Jean Giraudoux and André Maurois. The office in the Place de la Madeleine gradually became a model of efficiency, due mainly to young David Strathallan, now Lord Perth, who was intelligent, charming and a hard

worker, coupled with Noël's initial enthusiasm. They persevered but Maurois and Giraudoux evinced little interest in their endeavours beyond inviting them to dinner and discussing French and English literature. All his life any kind of pomposity provoked Noël's derision and to the 'Very Confidential' and 'Top Secret' labels on the despatches they received from England Noël soon began to add 'And *Very* Dull' which was only too true, for they invariably contained information he had already read in the *Continental Daily Mail* the day before. There was in fact very little to report, for these were the long months of the Phoney War, more aptly described by the French as *une drôle de guerre*. Noël and his staff tried hard to make a go of it and, in spite of many frustrations and the poor material at their disposal, they achieved a certain amount that was worthwhile.

Noël's disenchantment increased together with his boredom at the lack of action until he was given leave of absence by Sir Campbell to leave Paris for America in April 1940. No sooner was this permission given than the Nazis invaded Norway and Denmark, Chamberlain cheerfully and inaccurately announced that Hitler had missed the bus, and the tempo of the war quickened perceptibly. To Noël's surprise he was assured it was important that he should leave for America as arranged, keep his eyes and ears open and report back to London anything of interest. This he did. The Paris office was not disbanded until the Germans were almost at the gates

Noël's painting Junction Road *No. 3; the plate he designed for Royal Doulton; and his last Jamaican painting. One day, after gazing at this painting for a while, Coley turned to Noël and said: 'I've counted 242 people.' To which the Master replied: 'I must have painted 484 feet.'*

Above: In contrast, an English scene, Romney Marsh.

*Derek Hill at work: 'My eyes',
complained Noël, 'are too close
together', but it remains the most
alive of all the portraits. Left: The
finished work.*

*Lord Mountbatten, and the opening
lines of Noël's 'thank you' poem at
the end of his last wartime troop
tour, Ceylon July 1944:
It isn't for me
To bend the knee
And curtsey and cringe and pander
Because my Junior happens to be
A really Supreeme Commander.
But nevertheless
I must confess,
Dear Dickie, my stay in Kandy,
Apart from being a great success,
Has made me feel fine and dandy.*

*Opposite (l. to r.): Noël, Lord
Mountbatten, Graham, Oona
Chaplin, Lynn Fontanne and
Charles Chaplin; Coley, Noël, Peter
O'Toole and Graham; Natalie Wood,
David Niven, Noël, Sophia Loren
and David Jr.*

of the city, by which time, though he tried desperately to get there, he was too late and had to be diverted via Lisbon to London.

There followed weeks of indecision, but at last came a firm decision from Duff Cooper that he should return to America and carry on as before. This brought forth a long, loud howl of indignation from the British press: what was the frivolous Coward doing, conferring with President Roosevelt in the White House and making top-level decisions with the British Ambassador? (Paying a friendly visit or two with the former, and trying to start negotiations for the evacuation of the children of the Actor's Orphanage, of which Noël was President, with the latter.) While he was in Washington, Noël was invited by the Australian Minister, Richard Casey, to visit the Antipodes. He made eight major broadcasts on the British War Effort (later published as *Australia Visited*), gave as many concerts as he could to the troops in hospital or in training, which he did with conspicuous personal success, and also gave a series of concerts from which the Australian Red Cross greatly benefited financially. On his return to England, after nine months, in April 1941, he was interviewed by the British press *en masse* (he had made a rule to give them no interviews ever since the *Sirocco* disaster), faced his critics, and answered all their questions including one about the hoary old rumour that he had been seen flaunting naval uniform in Paris at the beginning of the war. 'Have you in fact ever worn uniform?' 'Yes, for three nights when I played in *Journey's End* in Singapore in 1930.'

Noël had made one last attempt to get an official war job a month before this while he was in New York. There he had met and become instant friends with Sir William Stephenson, head of British Intelligence in the USA, familiarly known as 'Little Bill' and in 1979 famous as the subject of the biography entitled *A Man Called Intrepid*. Little Bill had faith in Noël's integrity and his biography makes it clear that he also genuinely believed that Noël could have been useful in Intelligence. Noël's very notoriety, used openly, would have made a wonderful 'cover' – no need for cloak, dagger or dark glasses – but a 'Greater Power' (Churchill?) thought precisely the opposite. An official message read: 'Complete secrecy is the foundation of our work. The immense amount of publicity in British Press unfortunately makes entire scheme impracticable.' This was a great blow to Noël, who felt angry at being let down by people he had thought his

friends and then miserable at being unwanted and once more at a loose end. But not for long: he was nothing if not resilient. He put thoughts of an official post behind him for good and all, his disappointment receded and he had peace of mind at being home in England in spite of its war-time discomforts and shortages. After the turmoil of the past months he thought he deserved a rest and years later he wrote about the week's holiday he gave himself at Portmeirion in Wales:

I must say with what will seem to be a refreshing gust of modesty that in my opinion I have never achieved the perfect play I have always longed, and will always long, to write – but I shall ever be grateful for the almost psychic gift that enabled me to write *Blithe Spirit* in five days during one of the darkest years of the war. It was not meticulously constructed in advance and only one day elapsed between its original conception and the moment I sat down to write it. It fell into my mind and on to the manuscript. Six weeks later it was produced and ran for four and a half years, and I am still wondering whether or not it was 'Important'. Only time will tell.

Noël now determined that if he were going to make a contribution to the war effort it would have to be in his own field, that of entertainment, as Churchill had advised him from the start – though he wanted to make a *lasting* contribution and this would, therefore, have to be as a writer, not a performer. *Blithe Spirit* has proved to be lasting all right; he had got off to a good quick start. At this time he also began to keep a diary, scribbling down the events of the day in a kind of telegraphese before he went to sleep, and the entries for 1941 make evident how hard he worked to keep his vow to write not only a play but a patriotic song (*London Pride*, with the lyrics of which he had a hard struggle). Then, on 8 July: 'Suddenly thought

'The last time I saw Paris. . . .'
Noël's living room in the apartment at 22 Place Vendôme, painted by Catherine Serebriakoff.

Again on board ship, this time bound for New Zealand in November 1940, Noël faces the press; and on dry land, speaking at one of many engagements.

a naval film would be good from every point of view. Am thinking it over.' A few nights before Lord Mountbatten had, over dinner, 'told the whole story of the sinking of the *Kelly*. Absolutely heartbreaking, really magnificent. He told the whole saga without frills and with a sincerity that was very moving. He is a pretty wonderful man I think.'

For Noël to write a film script was an entirely new departure, but, undaunted, he worked daily for two months on *In Which We Serve*, until on 3 September he noted, 'Flushed with triumph at having completed script'. He was to have to rewrite and reconstruct the script many times before the film went into production, and there were many major setbacks and disappointments to be overcome before the film was finished and finally released to ecstatically good reviews. Through the good offices of Lord Mountbatten, and through him the encouragement of King George VI, Noël had, in spite of strong opposition from some quarters, enjoyed the full co-operation of the Admiralty during the film's making, but even this had been seriously endangered on two occasions. First came an outcry from the press, led by a headline in the *Express*, BATTLE OF NOËL: how dare Noël, the lightweight comedian, attempt to portray Lord Mountbatten in the leading part in a serious film about the Royal Navy in time of war? And then, on 16 October, in the middle of a script discussion, 'Cruelly interrupted by a shattering blow. Two police Inspectors arrived with two summonses from the Finance Defence Department. I am to appear before a Court and am liable to a fine of £22,000, apparently for having broken certain rules about which I knew nothing and now know very little ... Horrified and extremely angry. I shall be landed with a Press scandal which will be harmful to the film; this is grossly unfair. If I were not a celebrity, this could be dealt with quietly and quickly.' He was indeed technically guilty of not having declared his American holdings at the outbreak of war, but had been unaware of the existence of this ruling, though certainly his financial advisors must have known of it and should have dealt with it on his behalf. George Bernard Shaw most kindly wrote to him: 'There can be no guilt without intention ... Therefore let nothing induce you to plead Guilty. If your lawyers advise you to do so, tell them *I* advise you not to.' His lawyers strongly advised him to plead guilty, but he took Shaw's advice and in consequence had to face the music in the form of some stiff cross-examination in two separate cases resulting in fines of £200 and £1,600, respectively.

These tribulations might easily have endangered his relations with Lord Mountbatten and the Admiralty, and the adverse publicity might have placed the making of *In Which We Serve* in jeopardy. Noël had had many black moments ever since the film's inception, but Lord Mountbatten never failed him. Noël's tributes to 'Dickie' abound throughout that year's diary: 'Dined with Dickie. He was as usual wise, kind and stimulating. Know he will back me to the last ditch over anything'; 'More and more convinced that he is a great man. His judgement seems to me to be sound on every major issue'; 'Dickie's militant loyalty, moral courage and infinite capacity for taking pains, however busy, is one of the marvels of this unpleasant age. I would do anything for him at any time he asked me.'

Noël had insisted on his mother being evacuated to New York for safety at the beginning of the war, but after two years she began to pine to come home. Mrs Coward was now seventy-eight, the war seemed as though it would never end, and she longed to see England and her son once more before she died. After much influential pulling of strings and long delays she got back to London in July 1942. Her two great, immediate treats were for her to be given a special showing of a rough-cut of *In Which We Serve* and be taken to sit proudly in a box with her son to see *Blithe Spirit*. Most people saw *In Which We Serve* in those emotional days through a mist of tears, but Mrs Coward complained that it had upset her *too* much and as for *Blithe Spirit*, she hated it and told Noël that Jack Wilson's production in New York was far better – to Noël's fury.

Noël's next sizeable contribution to the war effort was to take out a company headed by himself, Joyce and Judy Campbell for a very long tour – six and a half months all told – of the major cities of Great Britain with three plays: *Blithe Spirit*, new to most of the provinces and, brand new because of their cancellation on the eve of the war, *Present Laughter* and *This Happy Breed*. In addition to this complicated repertory in austere wartime conditions, he and Judy undertook to give an average of four to six concerts a week in hospitals and munitions factories in each city, Judy bravely telling (sometimes bemused) workers in Glasgow or Hull while they ate their lunch about the nightingale that sang in Berkeley Square, and of how Arthur Murray had taught her to dance in a hurry. Noël sometimes had to shed his sophistication very quickly and switch to *If You Were The Only Girl In The World* and *There'll Always Be An England*, turning the concert into a nice sing-song. He also promised Naval Intelligence he would give a five minute security speech – 'Careless Talk Costs Lives' – after each performance; it was not easy to have to 'hold' an audience already anxious not to miss the last train or bus in dead of winter, but he did it. Discomforts apart, this tour was one of the most sustained and arduous he ever made, and in circumstances far removed from the familiar. Towards the end of it, in Aberdeen, he wrote:

Had an unaccountable come-over of nostalgia for Goldenhurst. So much another life does it seem that I can hardly believe those easy, luxurious days really belonged to me. I can feel myself now walking along from the garage on a moonlight night with the sea shimmering in the distance and the mist rising from the Marsh, letting myself in, turning out the one light, perhaps having a drink and a sandwich, then going upstairs to bed and lying in bed looking up at the beams. My own house. Oh dear it's all very sad. How fortunate that I haven't a real agonising sense of possession. If I had I should indeed be miserable now.

Banned by the BBC: the acid satire of Noël's 1943 song ('Let's help the dirty swine again/To occupy the Rhine again/But don't let's be beastly to the Hun') was lost on many listeners, who took the song to be a genuine plea for forgiveness of the Germans. Both the BBC and HMV suppressed the recording for several months, though at a party Churchill demanded three encores of it from Noël himself.

NOEL
COWARD
Flag-wag

NOEL COWARD MAKES HIS OWN CONTRIBUTION

TO THE PROBLEM OF HOW TO TREAT GERMANY

MONDAY night at 9.20. Priestley is on the Home Service programme. He talks about a place called Bad Tolz in Bavaria. He makes us feel the magic of this place in spring, in peacetime. Now it is the training school for the Waffen Storm Troopers, "the very cream of Nazi thugs and butchers." Priestley stresses the fact that these Storm Troopers are not only Germans but Dutchmen, Flemings, Swiss, Norwegians, Danes, Swedes, Finns, Estonians and Croats—anybody who will do the work of gangsterism. His point is that "Naziism is neither more nor less than a naked power system and not a truly national expression of anything at all." Of course, the Germans are a dangerous people, but they will be the ones to be shot down by these Waffen S.S. If we condemn them lock, stock and barrel, and leave it at that, it shows a superficial and unrealistic attitude of mind. "It is trying to solve the problems of 1943," he says—and as he draws near the end of his time we get ready to switch over, "with the ideas of 1843."

On the forces wave-length, at this moment, Noel Coward is singing. And this is what he sings: "Don't let's be beastly to the Germans, when our victory is ultimately won. It's just those nasty Nazis who persuaded them to fight, etc., etc." Can it be that the song was written in reply to Priestley? Can it be that it was timed to reach the air at this moment in reply to Priestley? And can it be that Priestley made this report in advance when he referred to the ideas of 1843? Is this the B.B.C.'s way of 'giving both sides'? The idea opens up new vistas of radio controversy.

The shooting of In Which We Serve,
for which Noël won a 1942 Oscar as
writer, co-director and star. Above:
Bernard Miles, Princess Marina
and Prince George (the then Duke
and Duchess of Kent), Lorn Lorraine
and her son Peter.

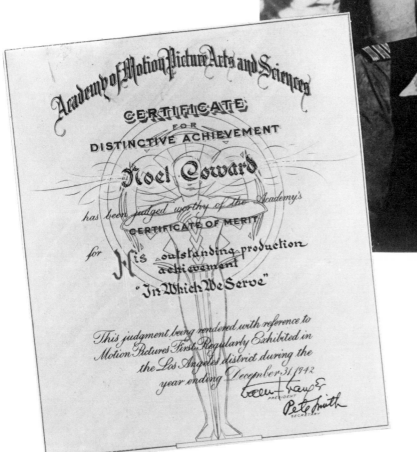

Top right: Poster for the film.
Opposite: Gladys Calthrop, David
Lean and Noël on the set.

But at the end of it all he could write that, though there had been many moments of exhaustion, bitter cold and near starvation, there had also been many compensations. They had been a happy company, with no scenes or squabbles from beginning to end. 'I wouldn't have missed those months of flogging through the provinces for anything in the world.'

Noël opened a season of *Present Laughter* alternating with *This Happy Breed* at the Haymarket Theatre in April 1943 to capacity audiences and paeans of praise from the critics. 'Everyone very gay owing to the rave notices of *Present Laughter*' and, next day, 'Matinée, packed house, wonderful audience. In the evening *Happy Breed* the same. Notices for *Happy Breed* wildly enthusiastic. It seems that I have progressed greatly as a writer because I have become so human! – this is a very interesting development. My comedy too is now on a level with the Restoration boys, so now I need never look back!' At the same time letters, cables and rave reviews were pouring in from all over the world for *In Which We Serve*, and *Blithe Spirit* was still running at the Duchess. Noël was riding high on a wave of success, prestige and popularity such as he had not enjoyed for many years. He was, in consequence, much in demand: everyone wanted him to 'tour and give concerts'.

Noël's travel urge and his continual quest for the sun had perforce been repressed for a long time, and he was only too willing to accept these

Blithe Spirit, the longest-running of all the Coward comedies, lasted 1,997 wartime performances; the original cast was headed by Kay Hammond, Fay Compton, Cecil Parker and Margaret Rutherford (opposite left) as Madame Arcati. Right and bottom left: A scene from the play.

Present Laughter and This Happy Breed, the two plays Noël had been rehearsing at the outbreak of war finally reached London in the spring of 1943 with Noël himself as director and star. Opposite below: With Joyce Carey in Present Laughter and in This Happy Breed.

NOEL COWARD
Master of the bubble

Noel Coward Gives the Navy a Song

Coward made tours to different fronts, and visits to the Navy. Other stars, having agreed to do ENSA work six weeks in the year, proved "not available" when ENSA wanted them.

Left: 'An endless succession of rehearsals, performances, press conferences, broadcasts, official luncheons, bazaar openings, dinners, arrivals, departures and civil receptions': the wartime troop tours that took Noël to South Africa, the Middle East and Australia/New Zealand also permitted the occasional moment on a beach.

invitations. First, as soon as he was free, he toured Gibraltar, North Africa, Malta and Egypt, a tour which resulted in the publication of *Middle East Diary*, which Noël intended to be a tribute to the men of the fighting forces he had met and entertained on his travels, but which pleased nobody. Ivor Brown wrote: 'He sees so much – and so little. He has travelled far more than most men of his age and yet when he writes, it always has to be of the same little world. Dump him anywhere . . . and he would certainly at once run into somebody known as Tim or Tiny, Boodles or Bims, and be dining with an Excellency or an Admiral twenty-minutes later.' Noël was in fact the least pompous man in the world, but the footnotes with which the book is disfigured (explaining that Boodles was Lieut-General the Hon. Sir Somebody Smythe-Something) give an effect of false grandeur – exactly the reverse of the easy, casual feeling he had hoped his day-to-day jottings would induce in the reader.

Noël sailed from Glasgow via New York for a concert tour of South Africa at the invitation of General Smuts, unaware of the antagonism *Middle East Diary* had caused. But ultimately the criticism had one lastingly good effect: he became conscious of the banality of the daily details in his diaries and instead kept a journal written when the events of the week had had time to establish in his mind their proper degree of importance. The daily chore thus became a weekly pleasure; he enjoyed the wider framework and happily wrote up his journal every Sunday morning for the rest of his life.

During his three months in South Africa Noël again started the gruelling routine he had already experienced for shorter periods in Australia and the Middle East: rehearsals, then the performances themselves, speeches at official luncheons and dinners, departures and arrivals with civic receptions, radio broadcasts, at all of which he was expected to be at the top of his form – the witty Noël Coward. The crowds were enormous wherever he went, with lines of police having to hold them back. The tour was so successful that towards the end of it, instead of coming home as he longed to do, he went at Lord Mountbatten's urgent request to the latter's HQ in Ceylon and from thence to entertain the Fourteenth – the 'Forgotten' – Army in Assam and Burma. This last gave him the deepest satisfaction of his whole war: at last he was in the front line, sometimes as near as four hundred yards or so from the Japanese,

THE NEW YORKER

One of America's least likely 'Bundles for Britain'.

"I thought somebody like Noel Coward might be able to use it."

NO SIGHS IN NEW COWARD SHOW

by Beverley Nichols

Sigh No More. *At the Piccadilly Theatre.*

IF I am offered champagne in these days I do not sniff at the vintage. I do not wrinkle a critical nostril and mutter " 1935 was a better year," or " Do you remember that magnum of Pommery '29 ? "

Coward is the champagne of the theatre.

It is conceivable, that somebody might construe this very obvious metaphor as a suggestion that he is all froth and bubbles. Such an interpretation would be an insult not only to Coward but to a very noble wine.

There is poetry in champagne. A high tradition and a delicate technique has gone to its making. It is an international wine — as generous as the sunshine w h i c h dances through it.

Many and varied are the occasions which its genius may accompany, from the cradle to the grave. Not for nothing has it been chosen to launch great ships as they sail out into the deep waters.

If you consider these qualities and apply them to Coward, I think you will find that they fit. The poetry, yes—the tradition and technique, certainly. Nor can we deny the versatility, nor the capacity to rise to great occasions. And always there is that incomparable tang, that subtly personal " bouquet," which is the secret of the Chateau Coward.

JOYCE GRENFELL, one of the stars in Noel Coward's new show, " Sigh No More," at the Piccadilly Theatre.

of a traditional air of old Provence, sung with perfect understanding by G r a h a m Payne—who seems to possess all the talents and most of the virtues, including modesty.

The wit? He has never written a wittier song than "Nina" a more devastating piece of characterisation than " Indian Army Officer," nor a more

Sigh No More *(1945), the last Coward revue and the one in which Graham Payn sang* Matelot.

seeing some action and giving five concerts a day at the height of the monsoon season to the war-weary, homesick troops, who were embittered at being neglected and forgotten even by ENSA. After a working fortnight in India and a farewell visit to Lord Mountbatten in Ceylon, he finally got back to London, having been away for almost a year.

On 23 October 1944 Winston Churchill, then Prime Minister, asked him to Chequers for a two-day visit. 'The PM was charming to me but looked rather tired. Heard at lunch the secret and utterly miserable news that my beloved *Charybdis* [of which ship he was the godfather] was sunk last night. Only a few survivors. I felt as though I had been kicked in the stomach. The Commander may be a survivor but doubt it; the Captain is gone definitely. That is the end of the happiest ship I have ever known. Tried to sleep but lay awake and visualised all my friends in *Charybdis* lying drowned and twisted and remembered every detail of the ship. Woke after a practically sleepless night with heaviness on my mind and talked to the PM, who was sitting up in bed. He thanked me touchingly for all I had been doing for the troops.'

Here ended, with all its excitements, dashed hopes and frustrations and its lasting achievements, Noël's four-year-long attempt to serve his country in the war. Victory was now within sight and he could return to the delights, for so long unenjoyed, of putting together songs and all the other material for a new revue. He chose Cyril Ritchard, Madge Elliott, Joyce Grenfell and Graham Payn to appear in it and they opened at the Piccadilly Theatre with the title *Sigh No More*:

Sigh no more, sigh no more,
Grey clouds of sorrow fill the skies no more.
Cry no more, die no more,
Those little deaths at parting
New life and new love are starting.
Sing again, sing again,
The winter's over and it's spring again. . . .

As the Studio at Gerald Road had been made uninhabitable by a bomb blast, Noël had moved into the Savoy Hotel, where Lynn Fontanne and Alfred Lunt were also staying. He has left an account of the last hours of the war and the first hours of peace, 7 May 1945:

A day of extreme tension waiting for peace to be declared. Did a recording of the speech from *Cavalcade* for Gaumont British. Spent the afternoon on tenterhooks and painted a picture. All London tremulous for the great news. Went to bed and tried to sleep but people were roaring in the streets, so I went along to Lynn and Alfred's suite and we celebrated with gin and tears the end of five beastly years. VICTORY DAY. Went wandering through the crowds in the hot sunshine. Everyone good humoured and gay. The Prime Minister made a magnificent speech, simple, without boastfulness but full of deep pride. In the evening we all had cold food and drinks at Winifred's [Clemence Dane's – 'we' being Lilian Braithwaite, Joyce, Gladys, Lorn, Lynn and Alfred]. We listened to the King's broadcast, then Eisenhower, Monty and Alexander. Then with Lorn and Joyce walked down the Mall and stood outside Buckingham Palace which was floodlit [for the first time after years of blackout]. The crowd was stupendous. The King and Queen came out on the balcony and we all roared ourselves hoarse. After that I went to Chips Channon's Open House party which wasn't up to much. Walked home with Ivor Novello. I suppose this is the greatest day in our history. SECOND VE Day, slightly anti-climatic but gay by the evening. Lunched with Lorn and we rested our poor feet. My 'Victory' article appeared in the *Daily Mail* together with the King's speech and the Prime Minister's. Visited Mum. Went to Juliet Duff's for a drink and to see Georges Auric. Stayed to dine with Juliet and Desmond MacCarthy and took them to the Stage Door Canteen. Made a brief appearance and got a terrific ovation. After that I wandered by myself in the crowds and had a lovely time. I sat on a stone balustrade in Trafalgar Square for over an hour, signed a few autographs and watched London rejoicing. Nelson in his spotlight seemed to be watching too. Friendliness and kindness everywhere.'

After early disagreements, it is pleasant to be able to say that Winston Churchill had, over the last two years, become a fervent Noël Coward fan. He wept through several showings of *In Which We Serve*; he laughed so much at *Blithe Spirit* that he went with a large party to see it a second time; he gave Noël's recording of *London Pride* as presents to his friends, and twice went to see *Sigh No More*. Noël had written a very funny and (as was so often the case with him) prophetic song *Don't Let's Be Beastly To The Germans* which Mr Churchill enjoyed so much he made Noël play and sing it over and over again:

It was just those nasty Nazis who persuaded them to fight
And their Beethoven and Bach are really far worse than their bite.
Let's be meek to them
And turn the other cheek to them
And try to bring out their latent sense of fun.
Let's give them full air parity
And treat the rats with charity
But don't let's be beastly to the Hun.

Darling Kay and Little Lad
Do not think our manners bad
But we had to hit the hay
After an exhausting day

Darling little lad and Kay
Pray forgive us if we say
When you both have drunk and fed
Please go quietly to bed

Neither sing nor dance nor leap
Exercise some self control
Go to bed and go to sleep
Yours sincerely Cole and Nole

Noël eventually caused a nationwide furore by singing this for the BBC (though he tactfully substituted 'rats' for the originally written 'sods'); most listeners took it seriously, believing that he was genuinely pleading for forgiveness of the enemy. He was accused by the *Daily Herald* of 'appalling taste and mischievous disregard for public feeling', the BBC and HMV disowned and suppressed the recording for the time being, and even Mr Churchill – hugely as he had enjoyed it – sharply reminded Noël that Britain was now technically at peace with Germany, no longer at war, and he really must not sing it in public any more. It did, however, creep back into Noël's repertoire, 'sods' and all, to hilarious effect when he took to singing in cabaret at the Café de Paris.

The end of the war found Noël without a house in the country. His much-loved Goldenhurst had been requisitioned by the Army, who left it reasonably clean but never let him know they had left it at all. The gardens were a Pre-Raphaelite tangle of briars, tall weeds and strangling columbines, and the forty rooms looked desolately in need of repair and a lick of paint – 'all a bit heartbreaking', Noël wrote, 'but I pushed aside the ghosts. What is past is past.' It would have taken years, if ever, in those strict days of building permits and long delays to restore it to its former comfort and beauty, so he bought the lease of a smaller house, White Cliffs, which was dramatically placed at the very end of the long, seaweed-strewn beach at St Margaret's Bay near Dover. The white cliffs rose perpendicular to an immense height close by Noël's bedroom, the end wall of which was either lapped or bashed by the English Channel according to its whim. It was an exciting house in which to live and Noël loved the drama of it all, his especial pleasure being to watch the never-ending, ever-changing traffic of the Channel from his bed. Seagulls would fly into his room and be stupidly unable to find their way out again: one large gull spent the night mostly on Noël's head, the only perch on which it consented to fold its wings. It walked slowly out of the French windows next morning exhausted – though not as exhausted as Noël, who maintained he heard it telling its friends, 'You've no *idea* what I've been through!'

The house was soon made cheerful by the use of brightly coloured curtains, coupon-free, and the favourite pieces of furniture fished, after five long years, out of storage in Tankerton. The stream of friends began again to arrive for weekends as they had at Goldenhurst: the same stream, enriched by new friends made during and since the war – Eric Ambler, Ian Fleming, Ann Rothermere, Rosamond Lehmann, Derek Hill, Ginette Spanier, Nancy Spain, Jean-Pierre Aumont, Joseph Cotten. . . .

When Katharine Hepburn brought Spencer Tracy and Constance Collier in bitter November, Kate insisted on plunging with every indication of enjoyment into the icy waves crashing against the rocks below. Constance, who was getting on for eighty, almost blind and walking with difficulty, bleated, 'Now I suppose we shall *all* have to dive in and save her.' Noël asked Constance if she was able to see what she was eating: 'Yes darling,' she moaned, 'but please don't give me white fish on a white plate.' Alfred Lunt, whose eyesight gave him almost as much trouble, exclaimed: 'Why, that's nothing. *I've* had to eat white fish on a white plate on a white tablecloth!'

Spencer Tracy, who had to drive back to London that evening, asked where the men's room was: 'When I was nine my mother told me always to "go" before leaving "then you won't have to ask to go on arrival". It's a good rule and I've followed it ever since.'

'You might well ask,' Noël said. 'You've been here since half past eleven this morning.'

From White Cliffs it was the easiest thing in the world to catch the Golden Arrow boat at nearby Dover and be in Paris in a few hours for

White Cliffs at St Margaret's Bay near Dover, where Noël lived while Goldenhurst recovered from its wartime occupation by the army. Kay Thompson and Graham Payn were regular, if noisy, visitors. Below: Joyce Carey, John Mills and Mary Hayley Bell with Noël.

A TRAVEL ASSOCIATION PICTURE
COPYRIGHT

Dear Noël Coward
Blanche Patch tells me
you have lost my photograph
and want me to replace it.
Here is the old blighter
as he is Today, superannuated
at 91½.

Ayot Saint Lawrence
9th December 1947.

Above: Bernard Shaw, Noël's original mentor back in the early 1920s (at the time of I'll Leave It To You), *came to his rescue again with valuable advice when Noël ran foul of wartime currency exchange regulations: 'There can be no guilt without intent,' wrote Shaw, 'so plead innocent.' Noël did.*

holidays, or to spend a few days at Noël's apartment in the Place Vendôme for what he called a *changement de décor*. Or even to pop across to Calais for the day to buy French cheeses and other delectables still unobtainable in rationed England. In consequence he got to know all the porters, stewards and other officials very well, all of whom soon became familiar friends. On the one and only occasion when he decided to smuggle forty pounds inside his socks he said to the man at the monetary checkpoint, '*Please* hurry up. All these banknotes in my shoes are giving my feet hell.' When the man at last stopped laughing, he said, 'Oh Mr Coward you are a card, always cracking a joke.'

Thanks to Tom Abell, head of HM Customs, and his wife Mary, Noël was given a front place at the dockside to watch Queen Juliana's arrival at Dover for a state visit to England. There was some confusion for a moment among the royal party as to whether Noël was there in an official capacity or not, and then Prince Bernhard smiled and waved and the Duke of Gloucester fell about with laughter at the muddle. The next night at the ball at Buckingham Palace Noël was sent for to dance with Queen Juliana who, as he put it, is no sylph, and they whirled so rapidly to a Viennese waltz that he began to feel dizzy, nearly fell over and suggested they should reverse. 'You mean we must go backvards?' asked the Queen and this they did. To Noël's horror there was an encore which he thought was never going to end, increasing and increasing in tempo until he felt sure he would faint and drag the Queen of the Netherlands to the floor. He only just survived, and he reported that the King and Queen were sweet to him and solicitous, but a little later the King confessed that he had done it on purpose, wickedly asking for the encore and urging the band to play faster and faster.

Noël had been working on the music, lyrics and book for *Pacific 1860*, the musical which was to re-open Drury Lane and in which Mary Martin was to star with Graham Payn as her leading man. So, of course, Mary came to White Cliffs, bringing her husband Richard Halliday with her and their pretty little daughter Heller. Heller was barely four and the tough-sounding American that sprang from her baby lips made everything she said seem funny: when Noël enquired how she had slept, she came back with 'Lika hunka lead'. And she appreciated the joke as keenly as everybody else when Mary bade her go and kiss Uncle Noël 'and say good-night nicely. Because if you don't, mother's going to kick your teeth in'. Everywhere that Mary went 'The Rug' was sure to go and, of course, she brought it with her to White Cliffs. She tells the enthralling history of The Rug in her own good book on needlepoint: knowing nothing whatever about the subject, she embarked on this huge and complicated piece of work and, being Mary, was determined to finish it. Noël said he was already sick to death of it. It took years to make and came to an exciting finish while Mary was back in London in *South Pacific*. She had only a few more stitches to work, when a message came to her dressing room to say that Princess Margaret was in front and Noël would bring her backstage after the show. How thrilling that after all its adventures a Princess should be the first to step on The Rug! Champagne was on ice and The Rug in place when Mary opened the door. Before Princess Margaret could enter Noël looked down and wailed, 'Oh no, no, – NOT that bloody rug again!'

We, the authors of this book, begin to feel that it is high time we introduced ourselves into its narrative. Two of us were by this time a permanent part of Noël's life. Since there are three of us, the only way we shall be able to write about ourselves is, fittingly enough, in the third person. Coley should have put in an appearance long ago, in 1936, when he

Graham. Noël Coley

A friendship of more than thirty years: Graham, Noël and Coley in their Astaire days – their faces at the age of sixteen were superimposed – and outside Montreux Casino in 1967.

At the Carlton in Cannes, 1946: Arthur Macrae, Paul-Emile Seidmann, Graham, Ginette Spanier, Noël and Joyce Carey.

first went to work for Noël at the age of twenty-seven. The first long period of time he spent with Noël was during the sometimes difficult eight months of the office in Paris, when Noël was without any other of his immediate circle. This inevitably brought them closer together. By the time of which we are writing, after a separation of four years while he was in the Royal Air Force, Coley had become a friend as well as an employee; they happily spent most of their leisure hours in each other's company.

Noël loved to recall that his first surprised sight of Graham had been at an audition for *Words And Music* at the age of fourteen, singing *Nearer My God To Thee* in a boyish treble and blending it with a tap-dance. Noël was so taken aback by this display of versatility that he engaged him on the spot. Fourteen more years elapsed before his real friendship with Noël began and grew into a lasting relationship. This took place during the run of *Sigh No More*: Noël wrote *Matelot* especially for him, and *Matelot* remains the most enduring and fondly remembered song from the show. He was to appear in three more of Noël's musicals, the next being *Pacific 1860* at Drury Lane with Mary Martin, by which time he had become a much-loved friend. 'I have many friends who I love dearly', Noël wrote, 'but all my life I've been able to count the ones who matter the most on the fingers of one hand': what he liked to call his 'family' had by now taken permanent shape and consisted of just that number – Lornie, Gladys, Joyce, Coley and Graham.

Sheridan will have to wait another six years until he meets Noël for the first time, when, at the age of eleven lunching with his mother at the Mitre Hotel in Oxford, they were joined by Noël and Coley and went to see his beautiful and adored grandmother Gladys Cooper playing a matinée of

Noël's comedy *Relative Values* at the New Theatre. Eighteen years after that, Sheridan undertook the difficult task of writing the first authorized biography of Noel, *A Talent To Amuse* – difficult, because he had to write it under the vigilant eye of the Master, which Noël admitted made for a tricky situation. But Noël never tried to influence the book and Sheridan ended up by earning his benevolent approbation, which happy conclusion was celebrated by Noël becoming godfather to Sheridan's son Hugo.

Noël and Graham gave themselves a holiday in the summer of 1946, before starting work on *Pacific 1860*, at Val d'Esquières in the South of France from whence Noël wrote one of his Fractured French letters to Coley (Cole had of course become 'Charbon' and his preoccupation with money was caused by the tiny travel allowance in force since the war):

Charbon bien aimé, Ta lettre m'a donné de la joie sans pareil; to begin with, like so many pleasant things, it was nice and long. Yes, please, I think it would be a good idea for you to round up all the dough you can, even if we don't use it all we can do some tidying up of the appartement [in Paris] and put the rest in the placard contre un jour pleuvant. We went over to Cannes on Thursday to see Arthur Macrae, stayed a couple of nights and it was verree verree gay and bloodee bloodee expensive. However, God looked out from the ciel, gave me a ravishing smile and deux cadeaux. The first was that we went to call on Maxine Elliott's old Fanny and she is letting us have the two best guest rooms at Château de l'Horizon, all for rien du tout. There is no telephone but we are using the Carlton, Cannes, as Post Office. So we are really sur velour. The second cadeau de Dieu was that, when I was girding my loins preparatory to panting round Cannes to find someone to lend me argent, I popped into the Casino, won eighty pounds in an hour and a half and popped out again! Le brave MG has been un ange – la vie est belle – Graham is Charbon-black et so is joli Maître. The Windsors are well and send you their love. The English visitors on the Côte d'Azur have come straight as a die from La Route Vieux Kent. Mille mille embrasses.

Maître.

It must be noted that during the visit to his old friend Arthur Macrae, Ginette Spanier and her husband, Paul-Emile Seidmann, materialized and were to play a large part in Noël's life from that meeting on. The immediate attraction Noël felt towards them was enhanced by his longing to know what their lives had been like – Jewish and on the run from the Nazis in occupied France since their marriage at the beginning of the war. He bombarded them with questions, wanting to know not only the perils and hair's-breadth escapes but also the day-to-day details of their hunted lives under the occupation. This deep interest of Noël's greatly helped towards the publication of Ginette's autobiographical *Long Road To Freedom*. A visit to the Seidmann apartment on the Avenue Marceau soon became imperative on the first evening of Noël's and every other stage or film star's arrival in Paris: a haven of anonymity, where they could relax in a welcoming ambience, safe from the demands of the Press. For the benefit of future readers of Noël's journals, and letters between him and Vivien Leigh or Laurence Olivier, it should be explained that Noël said of Paul-Emile: 'He's got one of those double French names. You know, like Marie-Antoinette', by which name he was known for a while. Then Ginette's somewhat exaggerated pronunciation of his name took hold, and he was known – and written about – always, as Polly Mill.

Pacific 1860 was one of the saddest disappointments that Noël had to bear – he had rightly been proud of the richly romantic score and lyrics over which he had lovingly worked for more than a year, but everything conspired against the success of the production: a crippling lack of sufficient time for rehearsals or necessary reconstructions, due to bomb-

NOEL COWARD

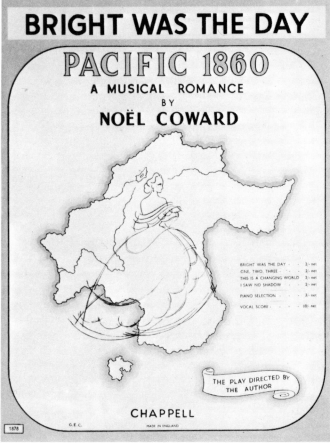

Pacific 1860, the Coward musical that reopened Drury Lane after the war: Mary Martin and Graham Payn starred, though only for a few weeks. 'It was', recalled Noël later, 'more a convulsive stagger than a run.'

damage repairs being carried out at the Drury Lane theatre until the last minute, and the lack of heating in the vast theatre during one of the iciest winters for years. The list of frustrations, quarrels and dashed hopes is endless, but perhaps the chief blame lay with Noël's rather milk-and-water script, which pleased neither the critics nor the shivering public who came to see it for four months, wearing thick coats and rugs over their knees. Noël mourned the lack of success of 'my poor old *Pacific 1860*' always, but a revival of *Present Laughter* at the Haymarket that summer with himself in the lead brought him more immediate comfort by playing to absolute capacity throughout the three-month season.

In January 1948 Noël took Lornie with him – her first visit to America – in order to see Gertie and Graham in the revival of *Tonight At 8.30*, which was then playing in San Francisco. They stopped off in New York and their three days there are best described in the following letter to Coley. (Valentina was the distinguished dress designer and Fanny Holtzmann was the most famous woman lawyer in America, a friend of Noël's and an even closer friend and financial adviser of Gertie's. She and her brother David were at this time attorneys for both Gertie and Noël, and Fanny had been largely instrumental in setting up this present production of *Tonight At 8.30*. However bitterly Noël may complain about her never drawing breath, it should be borne in mind that he would always end up by saying, 'I'm really very fond of old Fanny'. Noël had only just rediscovered, after twenty-odd years, the joys of buying clothes ready-made.)

In ze train for Chicago. Dearest Tole. Here we are bumbling along towards the divine breezy city, having got on the train with a maximum of effort and agony last night at 11.30. It is all very convenient and I am – 'ow you say – very 'appee. I talked to Little Lad [Graham] twice from New York and he was as bright as a bee and full of his press notices and his success mad. We [Lornie and Noël] had a gay time in New York and saw *Brigadoon* which I enjoyed much more the second time; *Antony and Cleopatra* was a wonderful production with Kit [Katharine Cornell] really remarkably good and Godfrey Tearle good too, but the tiniest bit trop vieux for Antony and rather handicapped by bearing a striking resemblance to the late President Roosevelt. Valentina had had a not very good idea about Cleo, that serpent of vieux Nile, wearing a series of housecoats with, as a sop to Egyptian tradition, a little diamanté insertion ici et la. I have a dreadful conviction that, though a great poet, Shakespeare's time sense was non-existent. It was all far, far, far too long. *A Streetcar Named Desire* is absolutely terrific, a moving sordid play superbly played and directed. It is a dainty study of constant nymphomania magnificently acted by Jessica Tandy. I have terrible visions of it being done in London by Coral Browne directed by Richard Bird! Leonora Corbett was very sweet and wicked, flaunting a new dress from Paris which I christened 'River stay 'way from my Dior'. Fanny Holtzmann has been driving me absolutely mad but is excessively efficient so que voulez-vous as we say in North Finchley. Mrs Loraine has taken to foreign travel like a canard to eau and goes about chatting to everybody and having a baleine of a time. We are due to arrive in Chicago in an hour or so, when we shall doubtless have a jolly little hashish party with Tallulah and be carried, swathed in sex dreams, on to the train for San Francisco.

Noël had first visited Jamaica back in 1944, stopping off on his way from New York for two weeks before tackling his concert tour of South Africa, and he never forgot the complete peace and rest he had experienced there. The visual memory of its beauty remained in his mind like a lodestar throughout the last years of the war to such an extent that he determined to return to Jamaica at the first opportunity. This cropped up in 1948: having learned that Goldeneye, Ian Fleming's house in the Parish of St Mary was available, he rented it for a six-week winter holiday in the sun. He found that he had not been mistaken: Jamaica was, if anything, even more lush and beautiful than he had remembered it, and he was enslaved by its charms until the end of his days. Ian's property included an idyllic cove with a beach of pale gold sand; the sea as far out as the reef had the prettiest tropical fish imaginable darting about heads of coral, while beyond the reef lurked barracudas and occasionally sharks – dangerous excitements which Noël revelled in. He made up his mind there and then that he must have such a dream house with a beach to match as quickly as possible. The land was found for it by Graham eight miles west along the coast at Port Maria; Ian's architects were charged to design the house and see that it was ready for occupation by the end of the year. He christened the property Blue Harbour, and shortly afterwards also found and bought another plot of land one thousand feet above it with a sensational view, the romantic ruin of an old Great House, and such verdant vegetation that at dusk the thickets lit up with the lights of a myriad fireflies. Look-out was the ancient name of this second property, soon changed by Noël once and for all to Firefly Hill. The glorious weather broke from time to time during the holiday; Noël grumbled, but in fact rather enjoyed the drama of it – the skies would change to battleship grey, then open to release a deluge of rain; there were black thunderstorms with Gustave Doré forks of lightning, and landslides and floods with telephone wires and poles blown down. 'A high wind in Jamaica all right, then next day a fantastically beautiful morning. Everything newly washed by the rain and the sea a steely peacock blue. Just the place for me!'

He rashly undertook, in the summer of 1948, the *tour de force* of playing the lengthy role of Garry Essendine in French for the Paris production of *Present Laughter* (known as *Joyeux Chagrins*) that autumn. The phenomenally smart first night audience consisted of equal parts of Paris *gratin* and the International Set, led by the Duke and Duchess of Windsor, with, amongst others, Susan Mary Alsop, who writes that she 'squirmed with misery – like having a friend do a recitation at dinner which flops. The audience sat like frozen mutton'. Noël, from his side of the footlights, said they were the most bloody awful audience he had ever played to. More appreciative audiences came in enough numbers to keep the play running through its promised season, but all the while Noël was longing to get back to Jamaica and the first sight of Blue Harbour, his new 'House Beautiful'.

Blue Harbour turned out to be hideous and his and Graham's first sight of it was a severe shock. The architects had not followed his idea of building on gentle levels to follow the land sloping towards the sea; instead, it stood up straight and tall, and was made even more gaunt by all its surrounding tropical bush having been cut down to expose a large expanse of almost barren rock. The interior had been hurriedly furnished by the agent with a result which Noël described as about as chic as the station waiting room in Hull. Much as he had loved his holiday at Ian Fleming's Goldeneye, he had been frightfully rude to Ian about the house itself, renaming it 'Golden Eye, Nose and Throat' or, because of the hardness of the beds, 'Bed and Board', and summing it up as 'perfectly ghastly'. Now it was Ian's turn to taunt Noël and this he did remorselessly, describing to others, in front of Noël, the hardships of being a house-guest or the horrors of having to lunch or dine at Blue Harbour. There was much of the schoolboy in both of them, and the abusive vendetta was really no more than a huge joke conducted for their own and their many mutual friends' amusement. Their staunch friendship remained unswerving until Ian's death.

The growth of vegetation in the tropics is so rapid that, as Noël said, 'all you have to do is plant something and then stand back', and Blue Harbour's nakedness was soon clothed in climbing bougainvillea and its bare garden covered with coconut palms, oleanders and hibiscus. As for the interior, 'let us aim for rough luxury' and in this he succeeded until, with the addition of a swimming pool with salt water pumped up from the sea, Blue Harbour eventually became his pride and joy, and a source of pleasure to the droves of friends who, for twenty-three years, came to spend their holidays there.

After the world-wide success of *In Which We Serve*, Noël and his team (of David Lean, Ronald Neame and Anthony Havelock-Allan) not unnaturally began to think of a follow-up or that there might even be several successful films just waiting to be made from the long list of Coward plays. Noël had proved with his script for *In Which We Serve* that he could write about the common man and woman (as opposed to his sophisticated and flippant Amandas and Elyots) with both understanding and tenderness. And Celia Johnson, who had been cast against many wiseacre's misgivings, because they said her face was unphotogenic, had proved that she was an ideal interpreter of these more 'ordinary' Coward heroines. She was, therefore, the natural choice for their next venture, *This Happy Breed*, in which she was called upon to play 'working class' comedy as well as the emotional aspect of a character for which she was already famous. She had, of course, been brilliantly playing both on the stage for years, but now she was playing to a much wider public and at the same time showing herself to be in command of the very different technique required for films.

In 1945, Celia and 'the team' reached their apotheosis with their third film, *Brief Encounter*, for which Noël made a perfect adaptation of his play

Canasta at White Cliffs with Joyce Carey and Ann and Ian Fleming, with Noël's advice to the new Mrs Fleming. It was the Flemings who encouraged Noël to revisit Jamaica. Below: Ian in Jamaica.

DON'T Annie, when playing Canasta
Produce a lip-stick from your 'sac'
And do up your face
With a roguish grimace
While giving dear Loelia the pack.

BRIEF ENCOUNTER

Miss Myrtle Bagot, at the Milford Junction refreshment bar, and Albert Godby, the porter, are concerned when Mrs. Laura Jesson gets something in her eye. A strange man, a doctor, takes the grit out for her.

(Eagle-Lion).
Director: David Lean.
British. Certificate "A"
Running time 85 minutes.
Based on the play by Noel Coward.

Laura meets the doctor again by accident the following week. It is the beginning of a sudden love that flares up in both of them. They meet secretly, but in the end the furtiveness is too much for them.

Rachmaninoff Concerto No. 2, played by Eileen Joyce, with the National Symphony Orchestra conducted by Muir Mathieson.

THE CAST

Laura Jesson	.. ..	Celia Johnson
Alec Harvey..	.. ..	Trevor Howard
Albert Godby	.. ..	Stanley Holloway
Myrtle Bagot	.. ..	Joyce Carey
Fred Jesson ..	.. ..	Cyril Raymond
Dolly Messiter	.. ..	Everley Gregg
Beryl Walters	.. ..	Margaret Barton
Stanley.. ..	.. ..	Dennis Harkin
Stephen Lynn	.. ..	Valentine Dyall
Mary Norton	.. ..	Marjorie Mars
Mrs. Rolandson ..	..	Nuna Davey
Woman Organist..	..	Irene Handl
Bill	.. ..	Edward Hodge
Johnnie..	.. ..	Sydney Bromley
Policeman	.. ..	Wilfred Babbage
Waitress	.. ..	Avis Scutt
Margaret	.. ..	Henrietta Vintcent
Bobbie ..	.. ..	Richard Thomas
Clergyman	.. ..	George V. Sheldon
Doctor	.. ..	Wally Bosco
Boatman	.. ..	Jack May

The last few precious moments together—Alec and Laura meet at the railway station, where they first met, to say goodbye. A garrulous acquaintance, Dolly Messiter, seats herself with them and they can say nothing to each other.

Laura returns to her loyal, devoted, reliable husband, Fred. And she finds reward for all she has given up in the life of which she is the centre, and in Fred's understanding.

Beautifully directed and intelligently acted, this is the story of a happily married woman's sudden love for a doctor, who returns her love, although he too is married. Their ecstatic happiness is continually pricked by their consciences, and the subtlety with which this is conveyed makes every scene ring true. It is tender, moving, pathetic, brilliantly handled by all concerned.

Brief Encounter, *an intriguing mixture of Noël's tight-lipped romanticism (it was based on one of his plays for* Tonight At 8.30) *and David Lean's early postwar realism; Celia Johnson and Trevor Howard starred in what remains a screen classic.*

'My poor old Astonished Heart' *(1949): an unsuccessful (at the time) attempt to lift another of the* Tonight At 8.30 *plays on to the screen. Celia Johnson and Margaret Leighton co-starred. Right: at the opening of the film of* This Happy Breed.

Still Life (in *Tonight At 8.30*), already a small masterpiece of economical writing. David Lean's sensitive, realistic direction, and the poignancy of Celia Johnson and Trevor Howard's acting brought forth rave reviews: C.A.Lejeune considered it to be 'not only the most mature work Mr Coward has yet prepared for the cinema, but one of the most emotionally honest and deeply satisfying films that have ever been made in this country'. Noël had so often been reproved for only being capable of writing about the useless froth of society; now he had the satisfaction of watching his compassionate love story of the provincial housewife and the young doctor become a classic over the years.

At about the time of which we are writing, 1949–50, he again turned one of his short plays, *The Astonished Heart*, into a film. In this he played the leading part of the psychiatrist unable to heal himself and chose not only Celia to play his wife, but also his other ideal partner, Margaret Leighton, to play the other woman. No one, since Gertrude Lawrence and Lynn Fontanne, ever gave him so much pleasure to act with as Celia and Margaret, or less trouble. By some extraordinary instinct they spoke his lines faultlessly – as Maggie Smith can do today – with every intonation magically right as far as he, the author, was concerned. *The Astonished Heart* was, however, far from being a success: it met with such abusive reviews in New York and London that it had to be thought of and written off as a total failure, best forgotten. Years went by until one evening on television Godfrey Winn promised Sir John Betjeman that he would make his wishes come true if Sir John would only express them. The latter, God bless him, said he would like to see again the love scene between Noël and Margaret Leighton in *The Astonished Heart*. Their acting was impeccable

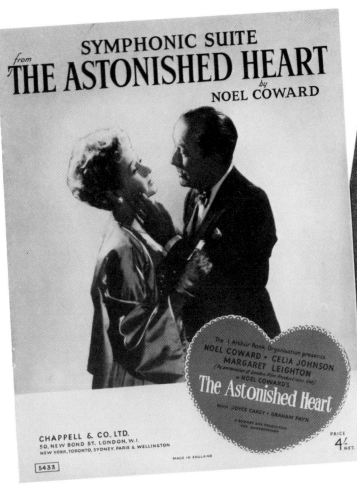

SYMPHONIC SUITE
from
THE ASTONISHED HEART
by
NOEL COWARD

The J Arthur Rank Organisation presents
NOEL COWARD · CELIA JOHNSON
MARGARET LEIGHTON
(By permission of London Film Productions Ltd)
in NOEL COWARD'S
The Astonished Heart
WITH JOYCE CAREY · GRAHAM PAYN
A SYDNEY BOX PRODUCTION
FOR GAINSBOROUGH

CHAPPELL & CO. LTD.
50, NEW BOND ST. LONDON, W.I.
NEW YORK, TORONTO, SYDNEY, PARIS & WELLINGTON
PRICE
4/- NET.
MADE IN ENGLAND
5433

MRS. CHURCHILL—
MRS. COWARD

Mrs. Churchill receiving a bouquet from Noel Coward's 81-year-old mother at the opening night of her son's new film "This Happy Breed" at the Gaumont, Haymarket.

and the scene, divorced from the story, was a strong one. This cheered Noël immensely and he said, 'Poor old *Astonished Heart*, I should love to see it again, just to find out if it really was as bad as they said it was.' He never did see it again, but now, years later still, it is beginning to be shown along with the three successful films already mentioned on late night television and in the art houses of the major cities of the United States. There has recently been a rash of showings of all four and – history up to its old trick of repeating itself – a consequent rash of reviews and letters from a whole new generation, who 'had no idea that Noël Coward wrote about ordinary people, and with such understanding, too'. One letter spoke for all: 'He evidently knew all there is to know about the hearts of human beings.'

*Pensively into the Fifties in his New York
East River apartment, formerly the
home of Alexander Woollcott.*

5
THE
FIFTIES

NEW YEAR'S DAY 1950. 'ANOTHER YEAR HAS GONE BY. A GOOD year on the whole. The half of the century and I am fifty years old! Fortunately during the last two weeks [he was off the demon alcohol] I have lost nearly a stone and have regained my figure and the shape of my face. I feel remarkably well.' The 1950s were to prove, as far as his private life, his finances and his professional appearances were concerned, to be one of the happiest decades of his life. He was much loved, popular wherever he went; he looked and felt younger than his years and was bursting with ideas for songs, plays, musicals, short stories, and even poetry – the latter a new and exciting adventure, though he was particularly careful not to refer to it as poetry or allow anyone else to do so: it was 'verse'. Throughout these ten years, only one major adjunct to his success was relentlessly denied him, and that was critical acclaim.

That is the overall picture, though it is true that to the younger generation of critics he was a has-been, an almost antiquated figure, who had enjoyed a marvellous heyday, now quite over. The kitchen sink was in and witty elegance was out. Starving tramps who were unable to communicate were all the rage, both on the stage and in the more critically praised films, especially if they were foreign. Noël stoically went to see, and sat through, most of these poignant entertainments, if only to find out how and why he was out of step – and besides, he didn't want to miss anything he had been assured was a beautiful and moving work of art. After much 'suffering', he finally evolved a theory that if you wrote a play or made a film about a crippled Mexican peasant shivering in rags and gnawing a dirty turnip in the gutter you were bound to be praised to the skies and awarded several international prizes. This theory was not too far-fetched, he insisted; he, at any rate, found it a great comfort and made a rigid rule to stay away from these masterpieces from then on.

It would be fatuous to deny that he was not painfully hurt by the critics' slings and arrows throughout this long period, and by the damning and, in some cases, abusive reception they gave to his plays. Of course he was hurt, and the disappointments were bitter. All the more bitter because the pattern was almost without exception mercilessly repeated: he always started work on the next production with the highest hopes, 'It's going to be one of the best things I've ever done,' and with any actor or actress only too eager to earn the kudos of appearing in the new Coward play, the whole enterprise would from the beginning emanate an aura of success. The production would then play to full and enthusiastic houses on the pre-London tour, culminating in an exciting first night in London with a packed and fashionable audience, often ending with many curtain calls and shouts of 'Bravo!' Next morning inevitably came the ice-cold douche of the critics' disapproval: patronizing notices, followed by more of the same in the Sunday papers and the weeklies. Hardest of all for him to bear were the pitying ones, more in sorrow than in anger at Noël's eclipse.

Yet, looking back on the Fifties with hindsight, Noël's plays didn't do so badly. First of all, in 1950, came *Ace Of Clubs*, a musical which, although not quite good enough, was perhaps ahead of its time: the English forerunner of *Guys And Dolls*, it had a plot full of tough chorus girls and gangsters, and abounded in good numbers. *Relative Values*, at the end of 1951, was definitely a success, with the incomparable Gladys Cooper giving a dazzling display of expert high-comedy acting, scoring a bull's-eye every time with her split-second delivery of Noël's funny lines. In fairness, we must mention that *Relative Values* got off to a flying start with excellent notices and enjoyed a very long run.

The London opening of *Quadrille* one year later was, on the other hand, for Noël a miserable affair. Six days before the first night at 'his and Gertie's' theatre, the Phoenix, he received the news of Gertie's death in the Stop Press section of an evening paper just as he was coming off the course after a carefree and lucky afternoon at Folkestone Races. The very last time he had appeared with her was when he replaced Graham, who was ill, for a few performances of *Tonight At 8.30* in San Francisco four years before and had found her as giving and generous to act with as ever, and her magic on the stage as potent. Only a few days earlier he had received a letter from her, her last words to him being: 'Oh dear – and it's you I always want to please more than ANYONE.' The next seven days were unrelievedly wretched for Noël, working on rehearsals and previews in the Phoenix, every corner of which was haunted for him by memories of Gertie. Worse still, he was puzzled and troubled at having received a marked lack of sympathy from, of all people, the Lunts. Binkie Beaumont finally explained that they, in any case on edge with an important first night imminently looming, had been deeply hurt to read in Noël's obituary notice of Gertie in the *Times*: 'No one I have ever known, however brilliant and however gifted, has contributed quite what she contributed to my work.' His journal entries for these days make unhappy reading: he got through the days 'somehow', including a seemingly

Ace of Clubs (1949), which was Guys and Dolls *a year or two before its time, and, because of its gangland theme, unacceptable to Coward audiences.*

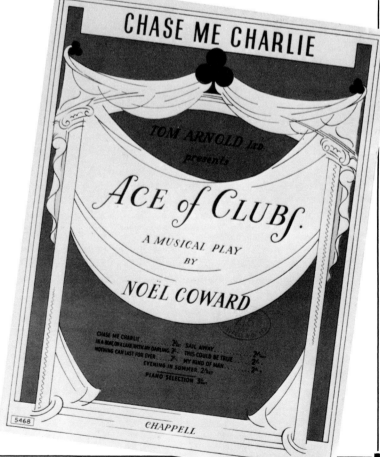

165

triumphant first night and a very glamorous party afterwards at Binkie's and then woke up next morning to find that, though the Lunts had been unanimously praised, his play had been 'viciously torn to pieces. I feel a terrible sadness inside. I suppose, with time, it will pass.'

Lynn and Alfred were immediately sympathetic, and the little rift was healed. Due to their drawing power, allied with their impeccable, richly romantic, star-sized performances and the beauty of the sets and clothes by Cecil Beaton at his best, *Quadrille* achieved respectably long runs both in London and New York.

To deal swiftly with the remaining three Coward productions of the Fifties: *After The Ball* came next, in 1954 – a charming musical adaptation of Oscar Wilde's *Lady Windermere's Fan*, but a not entirely happy marriage according to most reviewers, who felt that Noël had tried to be too funny at the expense of Oscar Wilde's play and the period. But *After The Ball* gave many people a great deal of pleasure with its lovely score sung with effortless ease by Vanessa Lee. Mary Ellis was dynamic in black velvet as Mrs Erlynne, and Irene Browne was splendidly regal and outrageous as the Duchess of Berwick. Then there was a little ballet, 'lyrical with happiness', danced by Graham and the very pretty Patricia Cree, which Noël had watched (with astonishment) Robert Helpmann create and choreograph in thirty-five minutes.

Noël did not have to put up with too many critical digs over *South Sea Bubble* in 1956 except for the usual comments 'superficial', 'hollow' and 'brittle', to which he wrote, 'I am *quite* accustomed', and Harold Hobson in the *Sunday Times* went so far as to call it 'the best play Noël Coward has written for a long time'. The public liked it anyway and adored Vivien Leigh, beautiful and shining with star quality, as the spirited and witty Lady Alexandra, and were pleasantly shocked by the sight of her getting very funnily drunk to the beat of jungle drums towards the end of act two.

Commercially, and from the public's point of view, *Nude With Violin* was the biggest success of all these plays. It was a comedy poking fun at 'modern' art, the writing of which, there is hardly need to say, gave Noël much sly pleasure and amusement. The leading part of the butler, a rather shady but resourceful and attractive character, was played by a succession of stars: Sir John Gielgud to begin with, followed by Michael Wilding, who played to standing room only (he was headline news because of his recent divorce from Elizabeth Taylor), and then Sir Robert Helpmann. Noël himself played the rôle in New York with great *panache*.

It is pleasant to realize now that so many of Noël's plays did so well during the long years he was made to spend in the critical wilderness. The plays themselves don't seem to have suffered much; only Noël was wounded, at the time, by the critical barbs.

Noël had become President of the Actor's Orphanage in April 1934 and under his Presidency, plus a good committee and all-the-year-round devoted hard work by Lornie, the Orphanage came to be efficiently run and the children well-fed and better educated. The Theatrical Garden Party, on the proceeds of which the Orphanage greatly depended, although a worry and responsibility to organize each year, had always been a glamorous occasion, with Noël in a cut-away coat, top hat and chamois gloves escorting to all the tents and sideshows whichever top-line film star happened to be in London – Mary Pickford, Ann Harding, Miriam Hopkins – and one year Princess Marina, after which he would sign autographs for money. But, in June 1951, Noël forsook his familiar role, really got down to work and gave a non-stop series of half-hour concerts with Norman Hackforth, his old friend and sympathetic accompanist at the piano, in a tent with a large placard advertising NOËL COWARD AT HOME. Noël and

Clifton Webb, Dorothy Dickson and Noël at his studio in Gerald Road, 1952. Below: Hatching a scheme with Hugh ('Binkie') Beaumont, once the most powerful of the West End managers.

Safer territory (left): Quadrille *(1952) was the last of the plays Noël wrote for the Lunts. Tynan didn't care for it ('Oscar Wilde rewritten on a Sunday afternoon in a rectory garden by Amanda McKittrick Ross') but the Lunt–Coward partnership and a period setting guaranteed the play a healthy London run. The gorgeous sets and costumes were designed by Cecil Beaton.*

*'Though we all might enjoy
Seeing Helen of Troy
As a gay cabaret entertainer
I doubt that she could
Be one quarter as good
As our lovely, legendary Marlene.'*

Noël's introduction to Marlene's 1954 season at the Café de Paris (where he had already launched his own cabaret career) summarised a twenty-year friendship. *Above: Saying 'Cheese'. Below: At Les Avants, Noël and Marlene with Graham, Kay Thompson and Marti Stevens.*

Norman's long experience of troop concerts together during the war bore fruit: the concerts were a riot, and that particular afternoon produced unexpected and far-reaching consequences.

It so happened that Norman was also accompanying Beatrice Lillie, while she gave a season of cabaret at the Café de Paris that summer, and Noël naturally went to his old friend's first night. After the performance, over a drink with Norman and the management, Noël found himself persuaded – without much difficulty, for his own finances were at a low ebb – to try his luck with a four-week season at the Café that autumn for £750 a week.

At midnight on 29 October 1951 Noël descended the famous staircase at the Café de Paris (Kenneth Tynan says he thudded briskly) to a salvo of applause and cheers from an audience composed of *le tout Londres*, headed by Princess Margaret and Princess Marina; more than a few fellow actors had made a point of being there to watch and enjoy his downfall. Mr Tynan goes on to say:

If you wish to see Noël Coward whole, you must wait for his cabaret appearances. In these he is benign, though slightly flustered, as a cardinal might be who had been asked to participate in a frenetic tribal rite. As well as benevolence, there is exuberance: he is filled to the brim with a burning, bright *nostalgie de la boo-hoo*. Gracious, socially, as a royal bastard; tart, vocally, as a hollowed lemon – these are the signs by which we recognize him . . . balanced before the microphone on black-suede-clad feet . . . [he] set about showing us how these things should be done. In sadder numbers, his face tightened into that expression which Robert Benchley once labelled 'the dead albatross look'. Baring his teeth, as if unveiling some grotesque monument, and cooing like a baritone dove, he gave us *I'll See You Again* and other bat's-wing melodies of his youth. His face, with its jolly, leathery jaw, is still that of an enthusiast: there are no ashes in his work. His sense of humour is as ebullient as an oil-well. *Don't Put Your Daughter On The Stage Mrs Worthington* he

Nude With Violin (1956): John Gielgud, Joyce Carey and young John Sterland in Noël's 'modern art' comedy; later players of the Gielgud role included Michael Wilding, Robert Helpmann and (on Broadway) Noël himself.

now puts over with a venom redoubled by the years: 'That sufficed Mrs Worthington, *Chr-r-r-ist* Mrs Worthington . . .'. All the time the papal hands are at their task, affectionately soothing your too-kind applause. His head tilts back, his eyes narrow confidingly. . . . Amused by his own frolicsomeness, he sways from side to side, occasionally wagging a finger if your attention looks like wandering. If it is possible to romp fastidiously, that is what Coward does. . . . In Coward's case star quality is the ability to project, without effort, the shape and essence of an unique personality, which had never existed before him in print or paint. Even the youngest of us will know, in fifty year's time, precisely what we mean by 'a very Noël Coward sort of person'.

Noël was right back there, where he belonged, at the top with one of the biggest successes of his life: every night the crowded tables clamoured for more until, in the end, the management offered him a thousand pounds a week if he would extend his season by a further fortnight.

He had that summer tired of St Margaret's Bay's delights, one of which had now become a bore and a nuisance – 'a beach crowded with noisy *hoi polloi*' – and decided to return to the more spacious and tranquil pastures of Goldenhurst. His last performance at the Café coincided with his return there and also with another happy event. He came down the stairs at midnight on 15 December as usual, except that this time it was to the strains of *Happy Birthday*, to what he described as a sensationally good audience, who made him sing for an hour instead of his customary forty-five minutes, and then he drove through the night to arrive at Goldenhurst at dawn. He woke up to: 'Probably the nicest birthday I have ever had. The house and land seemed to envelop me in a warm and lovely welcome.' He spent the afternoon hanging pictures and at six had all his local friends in for drinks, then 'went to bed at ten o'clock with kidneys and bacon on a tray, deeply and profoundly happy. I am home again.'

He returned to the Café a year later to the same vociferous welcome and yet again in 1953, this time especially to help celebrate the Queen's Coronation, for which gala occasion he also appeared concurrently in *The*

Nudes without violins: Nancy Hamilton, Katharine Cornell, Guthrie McLintic, Noël and Graham.

Apple Cart, Shaw's play about the pleasures and responsibilities of monarchy. In this he was blissfully happy to be reunited and acting with his dear Margaret Leighton, and in it the majority agree that he gave one of his most mature performances, at times brilliantly funny and by the end very moving in the melancholy loneliness of kingship.

Mrs Coward reached the age of ninety in this same year of 1953. In addition to her many years of deafness, she now found she was increasingly unable to see; reading, her one remaining pleasure, was therefore now beyond her reach and more and more often she expressed a wish to die. 'I am tired of all this hanging about,' she would say. Noël wrote: 'I dread her dying, but I also long for it. I want to be near her when she does, just to hold her hand – she has held mine for fifty-three years.' His wish was granted on 30 June a year later. He happened to be in London: 'It was as I always hoped it would be. I was with her close, close, close until her last breath.' The last twenty years and more of his mother's life had been made comfortable by her son, and her pride in her son's achievements had brought her great happiness, hence it would have been unreasonable for Noël to grieve for her, and he did not. All the same, 'I shall never be without her in my deep mind,' he wrote, 'but I shall never see her again. Goodbye my darling.' Memories of his mother, not all of them unhappy, were to haunt his dreams for a long time afterwards.

The far-reaching consequences of that afternoon of concerts at the Theatrical Garden Party in 1951 began to manifest themselves during his fourth and last appearance at the Café de Paris in October 1954, when 'a character called Joe Glaser flew in from New York to sign me up for Las Vegas!' The financial results of the seasons at the Café alone had been immensely comforting to Noël at the time – and now, five weeks at Las Vegas at $35,000 a week would mean a substantial security he had never known before, and out of which he could easily afford the few thousand required to fulfil his dream of building his 'very own, ideal' house on his beloved Firefly Hill in Jamaica. And then, as a result of his success at Las Vegas, came three television spectaculars for CBS, which left him with the first capital he had ever possessed in his life – investments amounting to the best part of one hundred thousand pounds. After his long period of comparative non-success, it was brought home sharply to Noël that, for him, the really big money, plus much greater appreciation of his talents, was to be found not in England but outside it, and this led to the difficult and at that time painful decision to take up residence first in Bermuda and finally in Switzerland, away from the crippling tax demands which would have been made on him in Great Britain. And then, later still, because of these successes, a whole new career of enjoyable and well-paid film appearances opened before him. What a profitable afternoon that had been, back in 1951! The benefits that flowed and spread out from it were for Noël never-ending.

The Las Vegas adventure was one of the most surprising things that ever happened, not only to Noël but to everyone connected with him and it. Joe Glaser was himself a surprising man! Noël at first thought him a typical sharp, shrewd agent and then discovered that he was untypically kind and gentle, with charming manners. Noël's New York friends were startled that he should have allowed himself to be managed by Joe; when asked why he was delighted to learn that Joe's clients were predominantly, if not entirely, black entertainers and heavyweight boxers whose fights Joe promoted, Noël said, 'My heart and reason go out to him because he at least took the trouble to fly over to London and make me a concrete offer. I believe him to be honest according to his neon lights.'

Noël' surprise that audiences in the Nevada Desert packed the Desert Inn twice nightly, loved him and were 'on' to every sophisticated point in his songs, was only equalled by that of the owner, Wilbur Clark, who was bemused by what he had unleashed and enquired, 'Who is this guy? You must tell me all about him.' Noël wrote: 'The first night from the social-theatrical point of view was sensational. Frankie Sinatra chartered a special plane and brought Judy Garland, Humphrey Bogart, Betty Bacall, Joseph Cotten and Lenore, David Niven and Hjordis, etc. Then there were Joan Fontaine, Zsa Zsa Gabor, Peter Glenville, Larry Harvey, Jane Powell, Rosemary Clooney and Michael Wilding, etc. The noise was terrific. Paeans of praise have been lavished on me with the most heartwarming and uninhibited generosity. The press have been courteous and photographers insistent but considerate. The news has flashed round the world and there have been cables, telephone calls and great fuss. I was driven out into the bare desert and photographed for *Life* magazine in my dinner jacket, sipping a cup of tea. The temperature was 118°. It was all very funny and enjoyable. Let's hope the mood will last!' The mood lasted all right, until the season ended on 2 July. 'I am proud and pleased that I succeeded in doing what no one suspected I could, and that is to please the *ordinary* audiences; they were what really counted and their response was usually wonderful. How much I owe to all those troop concerts during the war. After them, everything is gravy. It has all been a triumphant adventure and I feel very happy.'

Together With Music three months later (Noël's first ever television appearance as an entertainer) was another unqualified triumph for him, and for Mary Martin. Mary and Noël had already given two riotous cabaret performances together some years before in London in aid of the Actor's

Revived to celebrate the Coronation: The Apple Cart, Theatre Royal, Haymarket, 1953. Noël as King Magnus, Margaret Leighton as Orinthia.

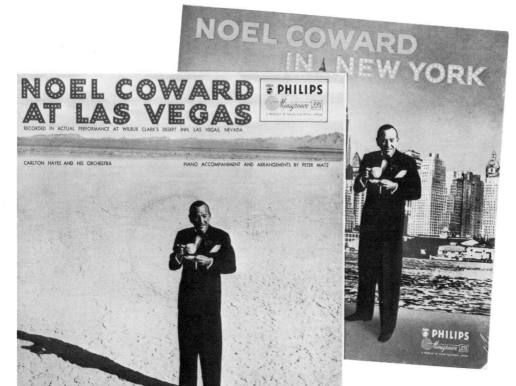

'Let's hope we have no worse to plague us/Than two shows a night at Las Vegas': Noël singing to the 'Nescafé Society' in 1955 for thirty-five thousand dollars a week. Johnnie Ray (above right) was once in the audience.

Right: On to Hollywood: Hjordis Niven, Jean Simmons, Greer Garson; and with Merle Oberon and Judy Garland after his live telecast of Blithe Spirit in 1956. Cartoon of Lauren Bacall as Elvira, Mildred Natwick as Madame Arcati and Claudette Colbert a somewhat forgetful Ruth ('I knew these lines backwards last night, Noël'; 'That, my dear, is the way you're saying them this morning.').

To Noël!
Blighely
Yours
ar auch!
[signature]

COWARD AMONG THE LADIES

Noël Coward, currently—as the U.S. columnists say—wowing them in Las Vegas cabaret, dashes over to Hollywood to greet some old friends at a party . . . in his own particular way: For Mrs. David Niven (above) there was . . . The Big Hello

an Simmons . . . there was g Uncle Noël Treatment

For Greer Garson . . . there was The Confidential . . .

176

Miss Martin, a needlepoint addict, immortalized one of Noël's earlier play titles as a token of their long, if sometimes stormy, friendship.

Orphanage, but this television spectacular was altogether a more important and ambitious project, involving months of painstaking rehearsal. Just the two of them sang, danced and entertained and, what is more, were televised *live* for no less than ninety minutes, a feat that is terrifying to think of even today, when such a show would be recorded beforehand, and which remains unequalled. They were both at the top of their very considerable form, vocally and in every other way. Fortunately, twenty-three years later, at the time of writing, DRG Records have rescued the sound track from what was believed to be oblivion and have issued *Together With Music* in a four-sided album, from which most of Mary and Noël's magic evening can be recaptured.

Noël's two remaining spectaculars for the CBS network – *Blithe Spirit* with Claudette Colbert, Lauren Bacall and himself, and *This Happy Breed* (in which he was reunited with his old friend from the long-ago days of *The Constant Nymph*, Edna Best) were made in the following year, 1956 – a tumultuous year for him, involving as it did his taking up residence in Bermuda on his lawyer's advice. 'You are your own factory,' Sir Dingwall Bateson said. 'You carry your factory in your head : what would happen if the factory failed to function and you became incapable of working any more?' He advised the move out of England, which would enable Noël to make his future financially secure. After much careful heart-searching and a storm of reproaches from some of his friends and later still from the British Press, he said, 'Dingo is right. I really *must* start to think about my old age, which begins next Tuesday.'

Increasing hostility of the British press: Noël's decision to live abroad (not – contrary to popular belief – to avoid tax but rather to safeguard his future at a time when it looked decidedly unprofitable), plus the sale of his houses and the opening of a series of critically unloved plays made the mid-1950s somewhat bleak.

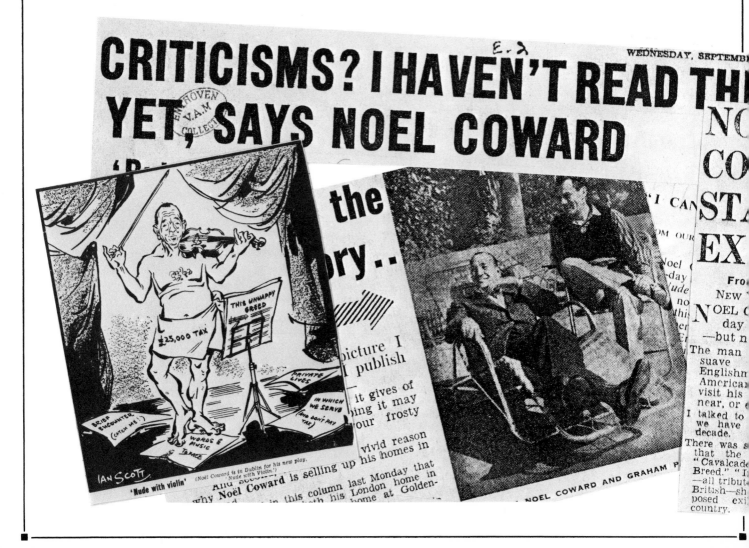

CRITICISMS? I HAVEN'T READ THI YET, SAYS NOEL COWARD

'Nude with violin' *(Noël Coward is in Dublin for his new play, 'Nude with Violin.')*

NOEL COWARD AND GRAHAM P

*The Master at the time
of his move to Bermuda.*

"I simply have to think about
my old age and about security
[Mr. Coward is 56]. British
taxes are iniquitous, quite an
impossible situation."

£20,000 taxes

If Noël Coward did go back to
England this year he would be
compelled to pay something
over £20,000 in taxes. By staying away, quite legally, he will
not have to pay the British
taxes.

But he will remain a British subject till the day he dies. He has
not given up England.

Some believe England has given
him up by a taxation system
which could have left the most
gifted Englishman in show
business practically broke by the
time he was 60.

He will not be at the London
opening of his play, "Nude With
Violin." But he said : "We have
a magnificent cast, so I feel
happy about it."

I first met Noël at his invitation.
We talked about England, and
have done over the years.

But today he did not want to talk
about England. He does not like
the way England has lately been
talking about him.

179

Firefly, high above Blue Harbour, Jamaica.

Richard Avedon photographed while photographing Noël for a legendary Tourist Board advertising campaign.

Life at Blue Harbour: (clockwise) Alec Guinness (sheltering from the sun, or else preparing for Lawrence of Arabia*); in a favourite straw hat; with Graham and Joyce Carey; on the steps at Firefly; sharing a joke with Graham; and Noël as Queen Victoria – not a role he ever played elsewhere – with Coley as John Brown.*

Clemence Dane at Blue Harbour and her celebrated head of Noël, later in the National Portrait Gallery.

Graham, Cecil Beaton (who took this delayed action photograph), Noël, Natasha Wilson and Ann Fleming at Blue Harbour. Ian Fleming below right.

Vivien Leigh, for whom Noël wrote
South Sea Bubble *(1956) and the*
English version of a Feydeau farce
Look After Lulu, *1959, with*
Anthony Quayle co-starring): *'a*
loving, generous and darling friend'.

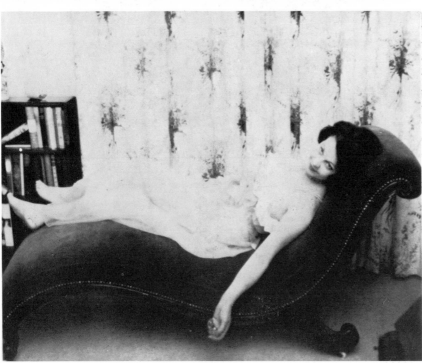

Vivien relaxing at Les Avants.

With Vivien Leigh, Kay Kendall and Lauren Bacall.

Cowardiana: a plate, his dressing-gown in a New York museum, and The Noël Coward Suite in the Oriental Hotel, Bangkok.

To Master Noel -- wee
box from
Lewis + Fluffy Damesy

Waiting in the Wings, *London 1960:*
Graham, Sybil Thorndike, Una
Venning and Mary Clare; Lewis
Casson was also in the cast. Dame
Sybil Thorndike signed the card
'Fluffy Damesy', Noël's nickname for
her because, he said, she always
fluffed her lines when he was with
her.

The Fifties also saw Noël's one and only excursion into ballet. His music for *London Morning* is charming, though his 'book' really isn't up to snuff and neither was the choreography. The 'other Noël Coward ballet', *The Grand Tour*, choreographed and devised by Joe Layton for the Royal Ballet and about to be revived by them, is a much more popular and successful affair. Set to the music of Noël's best-remembered tunes of the Twenties and Thirties, he and Gertie figure among the cast of characters, as do Mary Pickford, Douglas Fairbanks, Bernard Shaw and, either by chance or a predilection of Joe's for the name of Gertie, so do Gertrude Stein (with Miss Toklas, of course) and Gertrude Ederle, the hefty Channel swimmer.

Then, with *Around The World In Eighty Days*, Noël started the ball rolling for Mike Todd by agreeing to make a guest appearance in the film for the standard fee of a hundred pounds a day; Marlene Dietrich quickly followed suit and so did John Gielgud. With such an impressive start, Mike Todd had little difficulty in persuading other big names to do the same, until *Around The World* became one of the most star-studded films ever made and hugely successful. Out of gratitude to Noël, Mike Todd gave him a Bonnard as a Christmas present.

With *Our Man In Havana* in 1959, Noël started his new film career in earnest, playing Hawthorne the secret agent, one of the best and funniest character parts he ever played. Made from Graham Greene's famous novel of the same name, the cast list was impressive, headed by Sir Alec Guinness. Impressive, except for the role of Alec's daughter, which was given to a relatively unknown young American starlet who bore the Christian name of Jo and who fascinated them from the start by having her writing paper headed in gold lettering 'There's No Business Like Jo

London Morning, *1958: Noël's only ballet, written for Anton Dolin to celebrate the tenth anniversary of the Festival Ballet. With Noël and Dolin, John Gilpin at rehearsal, and Andre Prokovsky inspecting the Guards.*

Our Man in Havana.

Business'. She was evidently in awe at her luck in playing with two such eminent English actors, but had done her homework and told Noël how much she had admired his *Separate Lives*. 'I think you mean my *Private Tables*,' he corrected her, and she agreed. She was understandably bewildered by the correct usage of titles and felt that 'Sir Alec' sounded too familiar but got into a muddle over his surname and addressed him as 'Sir Gwines'. Later she took – perhaps because she was playing his daughter – to calling him Daddy-O. Noël was shocked, and Alec agreed with him that 'Sir Gwines' had sounded much more dignified.

Perhaps the most fortunate and lasting blessing of the Fifties came to Noël at the very end of that decade: through a chance advertisement in the *Daily Telegraph*, he found a spacious house at Les Avants in Switzerland, three thousand feet above Lake Geneva, in which to pass his remaining years in comfort with his collection of paintings, his library, which contained the books he had kept and loved since his childhood and youth, and all the other memorabilia of a full life. He often joked about his propensity for houses perched high, comparing himself in this respect with Ludwig of Bavaria. Sure enough, like his house on Firefly Hill in Jamaica, the Chalet Coward commands a glorious view, in this case across the wide lake to the French Alps soaring against the sky in the far distance. As this book is also about his friends, it is a pleasure to record that they came in droves to visit him in Les Avants, old friends and new, bringing him and themselves a happiness that can now be looked back upon with cheerful nostalgia.

The house is far from beautiful architecturally; Cecil Beaton's friends told him it might have been brought from Eastbourne, though Cecil found

With John Gielgud in Mike Todd's all-star extravaganza Around The World In 80 Days.

Some things never changed: the chair, the wings, the piano and the signed photographs were to travel with him from Kent and London through Jamaica and Bermuda to their final home at Les Avants. The second time that Noël and Coley visited the chalet high above Lac Leman having just bought it, they found it thickly wrapped in grey mountain mist: 'You couldn't see your thing in front of your face, even if you wanted to,' said Noël. 'Oh, my God, what have we done?' But the house was soon transformed into a happy and comfortable home, with lots of visitors.

it warm and comfortable within 'and it works'. Rebecca West also thought it had an odd air of Margate or Folkestone and that its white wooden balconies should have been hung with drying bathing dresses. In this she was curiously perceptive for it was part of the fun in the summer for Noël to take his guests to the swimming pool of the Casino at Montreux. Christmas and the New Year at Les Avants brought the contrasting delights of deep snow, which, once fallen, sparkled under blue skies and sunshine. The chalet might have been placed where it is expressly for Noël to enjoy his own version of winter sport: this consisted of getting himself and his guests on to small individual sleighs outside the front door, and then travelling at great speed down the drive, on to the road and round a sharp bend as far as the tiny railway station in the village. Joan Sutherland and Richard Bonynge in their adjoining property also invariably filled their house to overflowing at Christmas, and we would all join up at the station, pile ourselves and our sleighs on to the funicular and be conveyed to the hotel at the top of the little mountain at Sonloup, from which we would all come down again helter-skelter to the front door where we had started. This was even greater fun to do at night: to dine off cheese fondue in the hotel and then come racing down under a full moon, a sky full of stars, and lights twinkling from the chalets on the white mountainsides. Noël loved it, having been what he called 'a speed-merchant' all his life, but would

At Les Avants: Coley's painting of the chalet; Noël suffering from sunburn and tobogganing with Graham; Coley and Graham taking a bath together.

Opposite top left: Lady Diana Cooper. Top right: Rebecca West unhappy at the prospect of having her hair cut by Lynn Fontanne, who'd been eyeing her head for some time. Neighbours James Mason and Charles Chaplin with Noël at the Knie Circus in Vevey in October 1970, and Chaplin's entry in Noël's visitors' book.

Always a Joy dear Noël

Chad

Oona Géraldine.

Happiest of Birthdays Noël

Next-door neighbours at Les Avants:
*Joan Sutherland, Richard Bonynge
and their son.*

*Opposite: Peter O'Toole declining
the demon drink; with Glynis Johns,
and Elizabeth Taylor; Evelyn Laye
about to have a massage from Jean-
René Huber; with Sophia Loren, and
Moura Lympany.*

*love from your
'nice neighbours'
Joan & Ricky*

complain regularly, 'I'm getting too old for such capers', and then do it all over again the following Christmas.

Boxing Day – known as 'Boxers with the Nivs' – was ritually spent with David and Hjordis Niven and their children and guests at their chalet near Gstaad, a happy bedlam of noisy annual reunions and exclamations of delight at the multitude of presents given and received.

The yearly pattern of Noël's life was now set for good: as soon after the New Year as possible he – with Graham and Coley – would exchange the cold of the remainder of the winter for the warm sunshine of Jamaica, and not return to Les Avants until well into May, to find the mountainsides still white, not with snow, but with wild narcissi.

With Coley and Graham.

6
DAD'S
RENAISSANCE

AM HAPPY AS A CLAM,' NOËL WROTE IN THE EARLY SIXTIES, 'staying for a week at the Astor Hotel.' 'How *can* you stay at the Astor', his smarter New York friends wanted to know, 'right over there on Broadway?' But that was the whole point: catching up on all the new shows and movies had always been and always would be for Noël the most important aspect of a visit to New York. He had always been a Broadway baby, ever since that poverty-stricken first visit in 1921 to prospect for gold and in the process learn to love the city. 'Noël made no kind of success on his first visit', Alfred Lunt wrote years afterwards, 'but he was very likeable and got to know a lot of theatre people.' Four years later, as we know, he himself had become a Broadway star with *The Vortex* and from that time on had enjoyed stardom and the affluence it brings. But for the next fifty years, from the luxury apartments and hotels in the East Fifties in which he stayed, he would still forever worry about 'getting across town. The curtain's at eight and there's bound to be traffic. We mustn't be late.' He wanted to be *there* with a friend or friends, and with enough time beforehand to enjoy a sliced grilled steak, salad and a jacket potato topped with sour cream and chives at Sardi's.

The downstairs room on the left at Sardi's, filled with theatrical and literary notabilities all known to one another, produced each night the exciting atmosphere of a surprise party. Film star friends returned from months away on location, introductions to new friends were made, old chums suddenly turned up, so that joyful cries of welcome, kisses and hugs – not always sincere – were obligatory and the table-hopping incessant all through dinner. The din, too, was unceasing. Then, suddenly, the numbers began to dwindle; in twos and threes the stars left for their dressing-rooms and the sacred rite of putting on their make-up, and for the other diners it was 'curtain time' to go to see the latest smash hit or to attend an important opening night. The party was over. But never mind: although Sardi's would be hushed, silent almost, for the next two and a half hours, one knew that another noisy, jolly party would begin at supper time – after the show.

So no wonder Noël was happy at the Astor and eventually mourned its disappearance from the Broadway scene – with no transport or traffic-jam problems, he could easily walk the few blocks to Sardi's and thence to the theatre, twice a day if he was on holiday and having one of his 'orgies of theatre-going'. Best of all he loved the slow stroll back to the Astor at nearly midnight, with the hundreds of rainbow neon signs flashing overhead and the packed pavements below, stopping to window-shop from time to time no matter how garish the window display, or perhaps treating himself to an ice cream in Jack Dempsey's. The latter only on condition he could have a window table from which to watch the ever-changing Broadway scene.

With his recent Las Vegas and television appearances, his face had become more famous than ever: people would stop to tell him how much they had admired him, how much pleasure he had given them, or ask for his autograph, always gladly given. These brief encounters pleased him, sometimes for the touchingly worded tributes paid him by the strangers, or for the unexpected things they said. One matron stopped him with, 'I know who *you* are. You're Cedric Hardwicke, aren't you?' 'Yes I am', Noël assured her, 'and I've been dead for the last three years.'

Above: With the Kennedys at Cape Cod in 1961.

With Margaret Mead on the David Frost Show:
David: Do you believe in God?
Noël: We've never been intimate, but I think perhaps we have a few things in common.

Right: With Felicia and Leonard after a Bernstein concert:
Noël: Yehudi came to play for us last week.
Leonard: Yehudi who?
Noël: Bankhead.

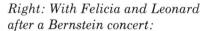

The record *Noël Coward In New York* includes a song with a verse:

> I like America
> I have played around
> Every slappy-happy hunting ground
> And I find America
> Okay.

(It also includes *Why Must The Show Go On?*, in which he dares to question one of the theatre's most hallowed traditions, and which caused Mrs Joyce Carhart to write when he died: 'Ah well, *life* must go on, if only for the pleasure of listening once more to Noël enquiring why the show must.') It was quite true: Noël did find America okay – in fact, he loved it. An eloquent expression of this love can be found in the 'Railway' speech from *Quadrille* beginning: 'It is a great territory, still untamed and rich with promise; even richer in variety. From the white frame houses of New England to the Florida swamps; from the painted streets of Charleston to the adobe villages of California, there is so much diversity, so much to fire your imagination. Oh Lord, the whole of life seems newly washed. . . .' In particular, though, he loved New York and he owed it much, especially for the generous and affectionate receptions he had received when appearing in his own plays on Broadway, *The Vortex, Private Lives, Tonight At 8.30*, and in the revue *This Year Of Grace*. And yet, he never entirely conquered Broadway with his operettes and musicals: even *Bitter-Sweet* back in 1929, though rapturously reviewed, ran for only 129 performances.

Thirty-one years later, however, ideas and songs began to burgeon for a musical with an American theme entitled *Sail Away*, and he confided to his journal that 'everybody seems to be enthusiastic, so I have decided to go blazing ahead with it and go into rehearsal next July!' He hoped he could pull it off, 'but if it flops, I shall still survive. It would and *will* be fun to do a nice big fat musical.' He did have fun; the lyrics and music came easily, and a little while after his sixty-first birthday he wrote: 'I must remember to count every happy day as a dividend. I've still got rhythm, I've got music, who could ask for anything more?'

The Sail Away *front cloth, and Noël promoting the show in the shop window of Lord & Taylor, New York.*
The last of the great Coward stars: Elaine Stritch.

Lord & Taylor
Fashion
Première

"Sail Away"
(our gear is stowed away, how about yours?)

Featuring:

Crystal chandeliers, Ninth Floor
Royal Leerdam crystal for two, Ninth Floor
Ottavia cloth, Ninth Floor
Altorr Sailfish, courtesy of Hilco Products
Grand Antique vynil tile, courtesy of Robbins

I'VE GOT A BROADWAY
HIT, SAYS NOEL

Rehearsing The Girl Who Came To Supper: *director Joe Layton, stars José Ferrer and Florence Henderson. Right: Tessie O'Shea in* The Girl Who Came To Supper, *Broadway, 1963.*

Below: High Spirits *in rehearsal, New York 1964: Tammy Grimes as Elvira, Bea Lillie as a prostrate Madame Arcati.*

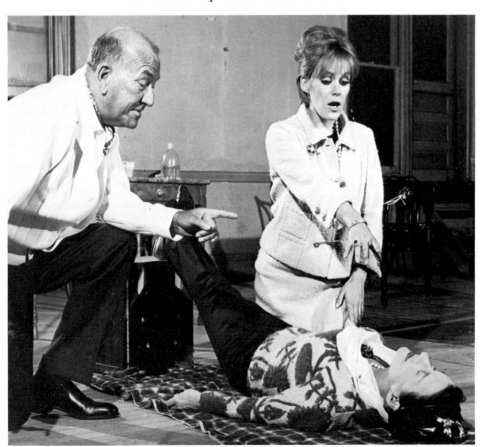

'Everybody' now began to prophesy that it would be madness to rehearse in the inferno heat of New York in July but Noël remained firm, wore a thin shirt and slacks, and cooled off after work by going to a movie: the cinemas, according to him, were air-conditioned to such an extreme that they were colder than Alaska. He was, in fact, thoroughly enjoying himself; the cast was (for the most part) youthful and (for the most part) happy as larks; and, apart from the dreadful drama of having to cut out one of the leading ladies and her role altogether, *Sail Away* was a very jolly show, enjoyed by almost all who saw it – except for the critics. It played to good houses for six months and then, like a flock of starlings that suddenly decides to fly off in another direction, nobody came at all. The same curious pattern was exactly repeated in London: 'too satirical for the general public' was the verdict of the people who should know, and they were probably right. After all the great expectations Noël had started out with, *Sail Away* did not take Broadway by storm, nor did it set the Thames on fire, but his songs and Elaine Stritch's mercurial star performance are still remembered.

Off and on throughout the next two years, 1963 and 1964, Noël was preoccupied with Broadway. His only professional connection with *The Girl Who Came To Supper* was that he supplied the music and lyrics, but he had so many friends on the production side and in the cast that his advice was sought and he was 'in' on everything. The late Harry Kurnitz wrote the book, based on Terence Rattigan's *The Sleeping Prince*. Harry was not

Cicely Courtneidge and Dennis Quilley in the London production of High Spirits.

Edith Evans and Maggie Smith in Hay Fever, *1964.*

lovely to look at, but he was a lovely, very witty man and a crony of Noël's. He once wrote a complete cast list of characters for an imaginary Restoration comedy, which Noël lost to his regret. The only character he remembered, or rather could never forget, was '*Scrotum: a wrinkled retainer*'. And so, although *The Girl Who Came To Supper* was not a success, the months of rehearsals, try-outs and previews gave Noël many happy times and much laughter, and *London*, the collective title for Tessie O'Shea's four cockney songs, stopped the show every night.

He then directed *High Spirits*, the musical adaptation by Hugh Martin and Timothy Gray of his own *Blithe Spirit*, starring Beatrice Lillie, Tammy Grimes and Edward Woodward. The Divine Grimes, as she was known, played Elvira divinely. Before she was engaged, another lady (who must perforce remain nameless) was suggested, to which suggestion Noël made one of his pronouncements, 'Elvira can be played in a number of ways. She cannot, however, be played by a camel with piles.'

Beattie – Noël never called her Bea throughout their long, close relationship – as he had predicted from the start, played Beatrice Lillie rather than Madame Arcati, with her unique and wildly funny (yet cool and inspired) genius, which was exactly what her adoring public expected and wanted, so the show was a success and ran for a year. *High Spirits* was, as it turned out, Noël's happy farewell to his musicals on Broadway.

'Dad's Renaissance', as Noël called it, really began late in 1963 with a revival of *Private Lives* by James Roose-Evans at what was then the Hampstead Theatre Club. The critics, especially the younger ones who had probably never seen it before, seemed astonished to find that here was 'the funniest play to have adorned the English Theatre in this century'. Noël, on holiday in Honolulu, was equally astonished to read the notices – 'It has suddenly been discovered after thirty-three years that it is a good play!' He found it highly satisfactory and 'a nice way to round off the dinner' that this had happened in Hampstead, where he had had his first great success with *The Vortex* so many years ago.

'So you've been nationalized at last,' Terence Rattigan exclaimed to Noël early in 1964, when Sir Laurence Olivier, Kenneth Tynan and John Dexter got together to offer him a production of *Hay Fever*, one of his earliest comedies, at the National Theatre. The play was brilliantly acted by an all-star cast headed by Dame Edith Evans, Maggie Smith and Lynn

Thank you so much
for giving up so much
of your time for us
to take these.

To Noël
from Tony

Above: Rehearsing Edith Evans for Hay Fever: *'The line, dear Edith, is "On a clear day you can see Marlow" not "On a very clear day you can see Marlow". On a very clear day you can see Marlowe* and *Beaumont* and *Fletcher.'*

Left: Noël and Laurence Olivier with all their yesterdays on the wall behind them.

Right: Dad's Renaissance. Noël back in London (Covent Garden) at the time of the National Theatre rehearsals for Hay Fever, *photographed by Lord Snowdon (who converted the well-known signature into a carriage and is seen at Les Avants).*

Montage by Cecil Beaton

Left: Angus McBean's composite picture of the three plays that made up Suite In Three Keys, *Noël's last London appearance: Lilli Palmer and Irene Worth co-starred (1966).*

Right: From one playwright to another: Maugham's inscription reads, 'For Noël, a picture of a gentleman on a shelf', a reference to the fact that his own popularity as a dramatist had waned in comparison with Noël's. Maugham was the inspiration for one of the plays in Suite In Three Keys.

For Noël a picture of a gentleman on a shelf

Redgrave, and directed by Noël. Its success caused many newspapers to say that this stamped him as a classic, but, as his major comedies had been in production somewhere in the world for well-nigh forty years already, it would be more accurate to say that this accolade consolidated their position among the English classics of this century. Noël ends a long and ecstatic entry in his journal with: 'The box office is besieged and I am very proud to be at the National Theatre.'

A reporter in Melbourne asked him, 'What is your idea of a perfect life?' 'Mine,' he replied. All the ambitions of his youth had been realized and he had emerged as an eminent national figure (the *New Statesman* even called him a national treasure), a grand old man of the Theatre, commanding respect for his long list of achievements and being accorded an almost awed reverence for his triumphant survival. What was there left for him to accomplish? Nothing really, except . . . For some time he had harboured a wistful and probably impossible dream of returning to make just one more appearance in the West End theatre, where he had started as a boy of eleven. A difficult dream to make come true, for if this was to be his swan-song then it must, simply must, be a success in a successful play. As time went by the wistfulness hardened into determination, and he made the decision to write effective star parts for himself in three plays under the overall title *Suite In Three Keys*. No stranger to hard work, he struggled bravely on with this task for nearly a year, hampered by a long bout of amoebic dysentery contracted in Bombay and which pursued its course through a long stay in the Seychelles. Too late he remembered Ian Fleming warning him years ago: 'Never have anything to do with the Indian Ocean. Everything is doubly dangerous.' The illness continued long after his return to Les Avants, including six weeks spent, dreadfully weakened and gaunt, in a clinic in Lausanne. His health now began a general deterioration: the arterio-sclerosis long before predicted by his doctors took hold and increased until walking became a slow, painful process.

Nevertheless, he would not give in, and in early 1966, putting on a brave show of restored good health, he flew to London and began rehearsals of *Suite In Three Keys* with Irene Worth and Lilli Palmer at the Queen's Theatre. Lilli and Irene, both fine actresses, were a joy to work with and proved themselves stalwart friends who never failed him throughout the run, especially over a new and, for Noël, mortifying difficulty: due to the arterio-sclerosis, for the first time he began to forget his lines. But they somehow always managed to 'cover up' for him. Towards the end, he admitted to feeling drained, exhausted and in pain – but proud to say that he had never missed a performance. His dream had come true to an extent even beyond what he had hoped for. Even the plays earned critical acclaim, as did Noël for his acting along with Irene and Lilli, and the public flocked to see what was indeed Noël's last appearance in the theatre. The old magic had worked, right up to the last. Peter Lewis in the *Daily Mail* wrote: 'As the curtain fell last night I felt oddly elated, as if I had recaptured the flavour of an elusive drink that one tasted when young but

Bottom left: With Elizabeth Taylor and Richard Burton on the set of Joseph Losey's Boom *(a film based on Tennessee Williams'* The Milk Train Doesn't Stop Here Any More) *for which Noël was cast as the Witch of Capri.*

Far left: With Sean Connery at the time of Dr No. *Left: Front cloth for the Tony Awards, New York, 1970. Below: With Cary Grant at the Tony Awards rehearsal.*

which had never been mixed quite right since. I know the name of it . . . not mannerism, not bravura, not histrionics, but style.'

Noël spent the next years happily enough, reunited with one of his oldest and dearest friends, Laurence Olivier, in the Otto Preminger film *Bunny Lake Is Missing*: with Elizabeth Taylor and Richard Burton in *Boom*, from a play by Tennessee Williams; and with a new but charming friend, Michael Caine, in *The Italian Job*. This was the last and – along with *Our Man In Havana* – the most popular of all the performances he had given in his film career.

In his leisure time he read and devoured huge quantities of books, including all the new ones, but returned often with profound pleasure to Dickens and Trollope and the reliable favourites of his youth. Also in large quantities he covered canvases with his brightly coloured paintings of Jamaica and the Jamaicans. After his rather slapdash earlier efforts, he began to paint with much more care and in greater detail. There is one big canvas of a beach scene with almost as many figures crowded on it as there are in Frith's *Derby Day* which he entitled *Two Nuns*, because there are two nuns in it along with the other two hundred and forty people.

Noël's seventieth birthday, the approach of which he had dreaded because he thought its importance (not of his making) had been blown up out of all proportion, became in the end a national celebration which he thoroughly enjoyed, with one or other of his plays or films on British television every night for the whole of 'Birthday Week'. At midnight on 15 December 1969 he came into his box in 'his' theatre, the Phoenix, to a packed audience of friends, headed by Princess Margaret, who gave him a standing ovation and so many loud cheers that the refrains of *Happy Birthday* from the orchestra were never heard at all. Then followed the midnight matinée with the stage filled again with his friends, most of them stars of the first magnitude from both sides of the Atlantic. The show itself (called *A Talent To Amuse* after the biography by Sheridan Morley published a few weeks earlier) was rehearsed and directed with such love and care by Wendy Toye and Martin Tickner that one felt it might have been a box-office hit which had been running smoothly for months.

Birthday Week ended with a huge dinner in the Lancaster Room at his favourite hotel, the Savoy, which was also televised nationwide and at which tributes were paid him by a great seaman, Lord Mountbatten, and a great actor, Lord Olivier. These pleased Noël perhaps most out of all the events of a week in which he had been showered with adulation and

A friend for more than thirty years. When the Queen Mother was laid low with a cold and thus unable to welcome him to Clarence House for his seventieth birthday luncheon, her message was that she hoped he would manage to make do with her daughters instead.

The finale of A Talent To Amuse, *Phoenix Theatre, London, 16 December 1969. Among those centre stage: Jessie Matthews, Edith Evans, Noël, Adrianne Allen, Gladys Cooper, Evelyn Laye and Anna Neagle.*

Left: Oh Coward!, *the Broadway anthology of his words and music by Roderick Cook in 1972, was the last show he ever saw there.*

"I CAME OUT HUMMING THE TUNES." —Noël Coward

Oh Coward!

Queen's Honors List Changes Name On the Marquee to 'Sir Noel Coward'

By GLORIA EMERSON
Special to The New York Times

LONDON, Thursday, Jan. 1— Noël Coward, the 70-year-old playwright, composer and actor who says he keeps fit on lots of aspirin and marrons glacés, received a knighthood on the New Year's honors lists issued today by Prime Minister Wilson.

Sir Noël, as he will be known, has written 27 plays and 281 songs, and a number of books too, during a career that began on the British stage more than half a century ago. His birthday on Dec. 16 was celebrated by so many television, radio and film revivals of his works that he cheerfully described it as "Holy Week."

Sir Noel plays it cool

SIR NOEL Coward emerged from Buckingham Palace yesterday, his top hat worn with a studied rakishness, and made quite clear that he was taking his new title very much in his stride.

With 16 other New Year Honours knights he had been invested and officially 'dubbed' Sir Noël.

He had the right to take two guests with him and chose actress playwright Joyce Carey and his stage and costume designer Gladys Calthrop.

Afterwards, he swept them both off to the Savoy for lunch. But, in his case, you could hardly call it a great celebration meal. He had silverside of beef from the trolley—no starter, nothing to follow.

But never a man to lag behind, he'd already had his celebration party. Without any of the publicity that surrounded his 70th birthday party in December, he had 100 guests at the Savoy last week.

affection in the form of letters, telegrams, flowers and presents from friends and admirers all over the world.

On 1 January 1970 the *New York Times* carried a banner headline QUEEN'S HONORS LIST CHANGES NAME ON THE MARQUEE TO SIR NOËL COWARD and continued: 'Noël Coward, the seventy-year-old playwright, composer and actor, who says he keeps fit on lots of aspirin and marrons glacés, received a knighthood. ...' The *Herald Tribune* said: A GREAT KNIGHT FOR THE THEATER – SIR NOËL and went on: 'At a dinner marking the seventieth birthday of actor-playwright-songwriter-wit Noël Coward in December a woman addressed him loudly as "Sir Noël". "A bit premature, madam," Mr Coward quipped. The joke ended today when the gap in the ranks of Britain's theatrical knights was filled.'

Noël was up and about early on the morning of his investiture on 3 February – too early, in fact, for there he was morning-coated, with silk top-hat at the ready, and with nothing to do until the car came for him in half an hour to take him to Buckingham Palace. 'Let's go through the mail,' he suggested to Coley and it was lucky he did, for among the letters was one from Dame Daphne du Maurier sending her love and congratulations and asking him to be sure to let her know what music they played when he went up to be dubbed. She said that the year before while she and Anna Neagle advanced, she wearing her blue dress from her daughter Tessa's wedding and Dame Anna dazzling in white, the music had changed when they were half-way, from *A Life On The Ocean Wave* to *Hello Dolly*. Like Dame Daphne, Noël had been fascinated by this particular haphazard chance ever since Larry Olivier had sworn to him that, as he had gone up to receive his knighthood, the band had played *The Donkey Serenade*. Of all unlikely pieces, the music played while Noël walked towards the Queen was Debussy's *Clair de Lune*. And yet the music was remarkably and touchingly apt. Noël had always loved it: when Jean Nohain had written the poem *J'ai regardé ce soir la carte de la France* specially for him, which he had recited frequently at wartime concerts for the Free French troops, he had always spoken the moving words to a softly played accompaniment of *Clair de Lune*.

On 14 January 1973 Noël made his last public appearance at a Gala Performance of the revue *Oh Coward!* at the New Theatre in New York. The revue had been brilliantly put together – as was *Cowardy Custard*, running simultaneously in London – from his own material. Every spoken word and every much-loved song was by Noël from the cornucopia of gifts he had showered on us all during his lifetime. The audience on this occasion, and at the big party afterwards, was again star- and celebrity-sprinkled, but in retrospect what makes it so moving is that by the good idea of using his Christmas card list as a basis for the invitations, so many of his old friends not in the public eye as headline-makers themselves were able to be there and be lovingly reunited with him.

Four days later, with Graham and Coley, Noël left for Jamaica and a long holiday in the sun.

Noël's friends were never far from his thoughts. Thinking of them, he wrote his last poem:

When I have fears, as Keats had fears,
Of the moment I'll cease to be
I console myself with vanished years
Remembered laughter, remembered tears,
And the peace of the changing sea.

When I feel sad, as Keats felt sad,
That my life is so nearly done
It gives me comfort to dwell upon
Remembered friends who are dead and gone
And the jokes we had and the fun.

How happy they are I cannot know,
But happy am I who loved them so.

Noël's grave in the garden of his hilltop home, Firefly,
now the property of the Jamaica National Trust.
Painting by Cole Lesley.

SIR NOEL COWARD
1899-1973

My mother knows Noel Coward